THE FREUD ANNIVERSARY
LECTURE SERIES
THE NEW YORK PSYCHOANALYTIC
INSTITUTE

THE FREUD ANNIVERSARY LECTURE SERIES

The New York Psychoanalytic Institute

THE QUEST FOR THE FATHER

A Study of the Darwin-Butler Controversy,
As a Contribution to the Understanding of
the Creative Individual

Phyllis Greenacre, M.D.
New York

INTERNATIONAL UNIVERSITIES PRESS, INC.

New York

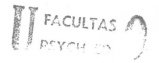

This is an expanded version of the Lecture given at
The New York Academy of Medicine, May 22, 1962.

Contents

Introduction

THE ROLE OF psychoanalysis in the investigation of creativity and creative individuals is not easily definable. It appears that the nucleus of creative ability may be in certain inborn qualities which are biologically given, and are beyond the scope of psychoanalytic research. Yet creative people possess much—including neurotic problems—not intrinsically different from those of the rest of mankind. The interplay of the neurotic developments with creative pressures and strivings may stimulate or interfere with the expression and fruition of creative abilities. This may tend to confuse the investigator, since in the one case neurosis may seem favorable to, and even appear to produce, the creativity, and in the other to destroy it. The study of the diverse forms of interaction in the gifted person can yield twofold benefits—increasing our insight into creative functioning and somewhat enhancing our understanding of the role of neurosis in various states of equilibrium or of imbalance. It does *not* attempt to fathom the ultimate source of creativity.

In this present study, as in certain earlier ones, the

clinical material is drawn from biographical explorations of famous people rather than from the personal psychoanalyses of gifted patients. There are certain advantages in this procedure. Based generally on examination of documents—autobiographies, memoirs, letters, diaries, and related records—of the famous person, it includes also the scrutiny of similar documents of his friends and other members of the family. In addition to these sources, his own creative products are available. The material thus studied is generally open to inspection of other investigators, who may then check the bases of the conclusions drawn by the psychoanalytic researcher. This accessibility of source material is possible only to a very limited extent with records of personal psychoanalyses, as it would inevitably risk a breach of confidence of the psychoanalytic patient, which might seriously hurt him and be a deterrent to other patients as well.

To be sure, in most instances a certain time distance must also be maintained between the psychobiographer and his subject, in order to avoid the danger of betraying not only the latter's confidences but those of others associated with him. He must in a sense have become a historical personage. This means some sacrifice of direct contact with people who have been close to him, and the loss of much fresh material in this way. On the other hand, if the subject has been a person to whom much controversy has been attached (and there are few famous people who have not been somewhat so beclouded), a lapse of time helps very much in settling the dust, and permits

[8]

the uncovering of avenues of study which would not be apparent during or soon after his lifetime.

It is customary to differentiate between primary and secondary source material: primary source material being that which is derived directly from the subject, and secondary source material that which comes filtered through the interpretation of others. In the first category are direct observations, recorded utterances, activities, and productions. In the second category are the biographies, memoirs, and critiques of his work—where in assessing the "facts" reported it is clearly necessary to consider the character of the interpreter, his personal relationship to the subject, and his own point of view in matters for which the subject is illustrious. In other words, the content of secondary source material nearly always represents the outcome of an interlacing of the character of the subject with some aspects of that of the recorder or researcher. There are few reports which do not contain implicit interpretation, be it only in the selection of what is considered worth reporting.

The distinction between the two types of source material is useful but not as clear-cut as it might at first seem to be, for few people are objective in their self-observation, and are even more prejudiced for or against themselves in their self-reporting. They are influenced by the images of what they would like to be—or in reverse by the sense of failure in not living up to their ideals. Moreover, there is usually the effect of a known or unknown recipient, whether this be the public in the case of published autobiographies, or some specific acquaintance or friend in the case of letters or memoranda. All this must be taken into consideration in piecing together the mosaic of fragments to make any understanding of the problems of an individual life possible.

It may be that these particular difficulties of fathoming the intricate and subtle depths of the inner man, and deciphering the significance of the patterns of his behavior and activities, are greater in the case of the creative person than in that of the less gifted one. The same basic patterns are there, but the variations and elaborations are more complicated— partly because the scope of vision and responsiveness is greater, but also because the creative person seems to have greater problems and greater potentialities of individuation and identity.

It is apparent that the psychoanalytic biographer approaches the study of his subject from vantage points precisely the opposite of those of the psycho- analytic therapist. The latter works largely through the medium of his gradually developing and concen- trating relationship with the patient who is seeking help and accepts the relationship for this purpose. The personal uninvolvement and neutrality of the therapist permit the patient to be drawn almost irre- sistibly into reproducing toward the analyst, in only slightly modified forms, the attitudes (and even their specific content) which have given rise to his difficul- ties. In this setting, the analyst can help the patient to become feelingly aware of the nature of his diffi- culties and to achieve a realignment of the conflict-

The Thesis

An INCIDENT in the development of scientific thought which occurred nearly a century ago forms the focus of this study. It was not in itself of major importance in its effect on the direction of scientific interests or theory. It appeared rather as a minor but prolonged squall in a particularly stormy season. This was the controversy which arose between Charles Darwin and Samuel Butler, in which Butler first enthusiastically embraced and then attacked Darwin's theories with bitterness and satirical fury, impugning his scientific and personal integrity. This unpleasantly dramatic incident holds our interest, however, since it appeared like a spontaneous experiment of nature, resulting from a special interplay of certain psychic forces and tendencies, which these two men possessed in common with other men—artists and scientists—of genius or talent. It was probably fanned into special intensity by the similarity of the backgrounds of the opponents and a degree of likeness in their personal conflicts, which were, however, handled quite differently by the two individuals.

The crux of the personal problems of the two may lie

in the especially strong ambivalence of their relationships to their fathers and grandfathers—a state of feeling which was more or less transferred to, and furnished the unique quality of, the quarrel between them. This, however, appeared and was believed by them to be purely on scientific and intellectual grounds. We shall concern ourselves with an examination of the vicissitudes and struggles of the oedipal relationship in these two creative individuals, especially the father-son rather than the mother-son part of it. Naturally the two aspects cannot be entirely separated. We are dealing especially with the eternal search for the father which goes on in many artists (using the term in its broader sense), and appears to be an integral part of their oedipal problems.[1]

But it is well to state again what we consider to be the characteristics of the creative person which then contribute to unusual preoccupations with and difficulties in the realizations of the creative person's oedipal strivings. These have already been enumerated in earlier papers (Greenacre, 1956).[2] A résumé may form the background for further discussion.

Most important is the deep sensitivity with responsiveness, the potential capacity for which is inborn. This sensitive responsiveness, which shows itself early, includes special awareness of form and rhythm, leading then to an unusual ability to perceive patterned relationships involving, among other things, special similarities and dissimilarities as these appear in the various media of sensibility. There is then an enlargement of the whole field of response, both in its extensiveness and in the subtleties of its complex rhythmic organization. The perception of objects and the relationship to them become endowed with a multiplicity of allied kindred forms: in our terminology, the *collective alternates* to the original objects. This leads to a multiplicity of experience with greater ease in and even necessity for symbolization and a richness in the texture and pile of the fabric of sensation. Expressed in other terms, the child with potential creative ability experiences deeper resonances and more overtones than does the less gifted child.

But there may also be an enhancement of certain problems. Basically this is due to the fact that the infinite increase in the inner and outer resources permits even the young child an escape from the personal exigencies in his development to the collective substitutes and the use of substituting fantasy as well. Even though he experiences changes and stresses of personal life poignantly and even drastically, still there may not be the same degree of obligatory settling of personal crises as may be true in the less gifted one. The turning from the personal to the collective may involve an attempt to solve the besetting personal problems in less personally stringent terms, or it may be a truer escape with the finding of other areas of immediate concern.

The readiness for contact with, and the capacity for using, the collective alternates tend then to permit a less decisive closing of the successive libidinal phases of early childhood than might otherwise be true. One result of this intrinsic state of affairs may be a diminished firmness of the barrier between primary-process and secondary-process thinking and imagery, a condition which seems characteristic of gifted individuals.

It is a psychoanalytic truism that poets and other artists know well and travel readily the high road to the Unconscious. They seem naturally to know and to use the language of dreams. What the analyst must work patiently to decipher with his patient, the artist knows and expresses. Yet paradoxically he is often unaware that he knows, at least in personal ways, what he may have expressed with beautiful conciseness in universal or collective terms. If we think of the creative product being achieved in part through "a regression in the service of the ego"—to use the concept of Ernst Kris (1952) [3]—we may well ask whether the tenuous character of the barrier between primary- and secondary-process thinking does not make regression extraordinarily easy in the creatively gifted person, and whether, indeed, he does not have so ready an access to primary-process thought, imagery, and relationships that his use of them is not truly a regression in the sense in which we ordinarily think of it. It seems rather that primary-process thought remains vitally present in the creative person, and is carried throughout life as part of the collective object relationships which do not have always to be sweepingly sacrificed to the personal. This continued access to states of early childhood may be the basis of the *innocence* of the artist, and his ability frequently to utilize the direct vision of the child. It may also contribute to the youthfulness which so many creative people seem to maintain even in personal expressions and behavior throughout their lives. In his discussion of Leonardo da Vinci, Freud (1910) summed this up in the sentence: "Indeed the great Leonardo remained like a child for the whole of his life in more than one way; it is said that all great men are bound to retain some infantile part."

It is impressive how many ecstatic states of early childhood are described in the autobiographies of creative people (Greenacre, 1956). The coloring of these goes much beyond that associated with the ordinary tendency to idealize childhood and repress memories of painful experiences. These recollections are almost surely screen memories but of a peculiarly exalted type. There are also descriptions of intense terror and horror, to be sure. But what is striking and characteristic is the prominence of mystical and religious coloring with the utilization of collective and cosmic themes. Also evident are the early seeds of exalted ambition and of profound guilt. All of this means that the oedipus complex too would tend to be acutely burdened and extraordinarily severe. No wonder, then, that the great artists, the creative geniuses, are the ones who have been repeatedly—almost continuously—absorbed in oedipal conflict, and that it is in one way and another the greatest theme in literature and in religion. The urge toward artistic creation seems to arise and be repeatedly associated with phallic urges in both men and women; and is inextricably bound up with phallic and oedipal problems.

The diffuse feeling of inspiration, perhaps better to be described as an intimation of inspiration, is characterized by a general sense of power and awareness reaching beyond the limits of the individual self —a haunting and compelling sense of boundlessness. Except for its greater intensity and its readier combination with the sense of vital natural and cosmic forces outside the self, it may not be very different in the gifted ones from the exhilaration in the phallic and early puberty periods in any case.

But the specific inspirational state as part of the creative process contains other elements and protean characteristics. Sometimes experienced as an actual visitation from a strength-giving supernatural source, it is likened to a mystical impregnation. The earlier phallic drive, disclaimed and allocated to a superior power, is superseded by a feeling of passive receptivity for new vitalization. There follows a sense of destined increase in driving power and of confidence in the possibility of entering new areas with new horizons. Specific inspirational states may involve, then, a temporary turning from an assertive masculine position to a receptive feminine one with a passive acceptance of the great gift of creation from the god-father, and an increase in power in this way. Or there may be a stronger retention of the masculine position through the gaining of permission from an all-powerful Father—a reinforcement—for penetration into the mysteries of the cosmic Mother.

In the need to generalize from a set of very complex situations, and to delineate the two main courses (the personal and the artistic) rather than to go at once into the interesting and diverse bypaths which both lead from and again connect them, a somewhat schematic presentation cannot be avoided. The experience of specific inspiration may seem to stress either masculine or feminine dominance in the inspired one. Such experiences also are frequently felt as though of great religious significance, even by those who have scant religious conviction.

The relation of these experiences to the oceanic feeling (Freud, 1930), presumably an affective memory trace of the infant's bliss at the mother's breast, is a connecting link in this picture with which little more can be done here than to indicate it. In any fuller presentation of inspiration, it should be given more attention. If the ideas regarding the general persistence of elements of the early libidinal phases are correct, it is not surprising that remnants of this archaic affective state from the oral phase might be more easily activated and color derivatives of later phases in the artist than in the less gifted one. Further considering the plasticity of masculine and feminine identifications in the experience of creative inspiraton, it is understandable that this may be possible because the increased sensitivity permits an unusual degree of projection of empathy to operate readily with both male and female forms, often supported by

[19]

vivid fantasy life. There is thus a predisposition to bisexual self-awareness, sometimes even producing personal confusion. Indeed, in studying the two poles of sexual identification in the experience of inspiration, it is necessary to see the connection of these with, and the influences arising from, individual special relationships with the actual parents. The question arises in every case how much the nature of the relation to the own parents influences the creative attitudes generally, and in what degree the latter may be isolated from the personal parts of the life.

Here, again, we would refer to Freud's study of Leonardo da Vinci, indicating that in that great genius there was not only the presence of this basic predisposition to bisexual identification but other severe complications of the psychosexual development. Inevitably a peculiar configuration of the oedipal conflict involving lack of adequate relationship and identification with the own father arose from the fact that Leonardo did not at all know his father until the postoedipal years. From birth until then, the fatherless illegitimate child was solely in the care of his mother. He was subsequently adopted by his own father and his father's wife, who had had no children. Thus the real mother was lost after an uncontested oedipal victory over a phantom father who then came to life, thus paradoxically fulfilling a possible family-romance fantasy in actual fact.

Freud points out that this unusual family configuration resulted in Leonardo's development of an appreciative but distantly cool adult relationship with both men and women; contributed further to his confusion of sexual orientation, especially as to the father's role in procreation; played a part in his probable commitment to life celibacy; and ultimately interfered with the full materialization of his genius (Freud, 1910). Did this not also influence Leonardo in his progressive interest in scientific researches and in his need to invent, and, further, in his unusual freedom from belief in Divine creation?

Certainly in all states of inspiration, whether in the specific, acute experience or in a subacute, prolonged sense of a compelling pressure toward artistic creation, there is an element of surrender to a power felt as though outside the self. If, in the personal life, fears of passivity associated with the idea of castration and reduction to a feminized position have developed, then the experience of inspiration and the development of artistic ability may be unacceptable and warded off as dangerous; or it may be rationalized as an actual religious experience. In either case, there is the possibility of sacrifice or distortion of creative work.

But to return to the main theme of this essay—the scope of responsiveness and intensity and expansiveness in the phallic urge is associated rather regularly with an increased oedipal drive and a corresponding increase in guilt and castration fear. A blocking of creative development may follow, with an intensification of morbid sadomasochistic drives and concerns. Under more favorable conditions, however, there is the choice between the normal route of resolution of the oedipal struggle (submission to frustration with subsequent identification with the father), and the more complex path of denying frustration and continuing the oedipal struggle with the aid of supporting fantasies. A varying proportion of energy may find its way from this personal struggle to the collective and be directed toward creative interests. It is probable that such a shift is much easier in the gifted person than in the less well endowed.

There is then the emergence of the fantasy of a godfather or powerful foster father replacing the own father, permitting and furthering the creative interests which are so closely allied to the hidden oedipal ones. In other words, a powerful and favorable family romance develops. This not only permits the gifted one to preserve his hidden oedipal drive, which is so related to his subjective sense of ability rather than sacrificing this to the overly strong castration fear. But it also alleviates the guilt for possession of capacity beyond that of the personal father.

But there is a penalty too. The deferment of the resolution of the oedipus complex may result in passive elements in the character being emphasized, and a repetitive, endless search for the ideal father sometimes becomes established. The fate of this must depend in some measure on the characters of those on whom this ideal is projected. But if there is to be the fullest fruition of the creative force, there must be a coming to terms with and inner acceptance of the creative ability as belonging to the individual himself. It is his own possession; his gift; his fate, burden, and obligation; not to be forgiven, sanctioned, or lightened by a hypothetical god or god-father.

In what degree such self-possession is attained must vary greatly. But its realization must continue if there is to be a freeing of creativity with the fullest growth in its expression, rather than faltering and blocking. Until it occurs, if it does, the creative person may split up his demand for a god-father or a father-god into different components. The search may continue as a hunt for a master, whether in the chosen field of creative endeavor, in economic support and shelter, or in personal contact and intimacy. At certain times and in certain cultures, such patronage was almost necessary for the artist's survival. That need for a total concentration on an inner content itself which is intermittently paramount, even at the expense of practical concern and awareness—the very quality of innocence—may require and attract such protection. But it is only when the creative person really acknowledges his own ability and accepts the responsibility that it entails, that there is any marked diminution in the dangerous guilt feelings and self-destructiveness. There may be a lessening of the dependence on a patron, and some tendency for the creative ability to be less influenced by other personal conflicts as well. These latter, however, are not necessarily resolved or even greatly relieved and are often seen to recur at intervals, even alternating with periods of great creative achievement.

The Controversy

In 1831, CHARLES DARWIN, a recent graduate of Cambridge, sailed on the *Beagle* as naturalist on a world-surveying trip. This was to last five years and have late but far-reaching effects on both biological and religious thought. Queen Victoria was then only twelve years old. Such world voyages were not very rare. Indeed, they seem a cross between the earlier adventures of discovery for territorial expansion and the ambitious cultural grand tours of the young gentleman. But in placing this time in American minds, we may remind ourselves that at the time of Darwin's birth, our country was only one generation past being a British colony. His actual birthdate, February 12, 1809, makes Darwin exactly contemporary with Abraham Lincoln; and the publication of the *Origin of Species* (1859) preceded our own Civil War by only two years. These two events, seemingly so different, are both in some degree manifestations of underlying related forces. But we turn now from thoughts of England and the United States, Darwin and Lincoln, to the specific controversy between Charles Darwin, the naturalist turned biologist, and Samuel Butler, writer, painter, composer, best known for his post-humously published novel *The Way of All Flesh*.

From the vast amount of reading necessary to give background and understand the content of the controversy itself, I am especially indebted to Basil Willey's Hibbart Lectures entitled *Darwin and Butler* (1959)[4] and to Clara Stillman's *Samuel Butler, a Mid-Victorian Modern* (1932).[5] The Willey lectures were written as part of a Centennial Celebration of the appearance of the *Origin of Species,* and deal exclusively with the points of controversy between the two men. The Stillman biography presents the controversy in its setting in the life of Butler. It was written at a time after the end of a period in the 1920s when Samuel Butler's popularity was at its height, and there had been a recrudescence of a defense of Lamarckianism. At this time, too, George Bernard Shaw had lent his pen to the support of Butler and Lamarck in his introduction to *Back to Methuselah* (1921), and even earlier in his preface to *Major Barbara* (1905).[6] In his 1921 attack on Darwin, Shaw referred to Natural Selection as "blasphemy . . . impossible to the spirits and souls of the religious," and wrote that "if it be accepted as a truth of science, then the stars of heaven, the showers and dew, the winter and summer, the fire and heat, the mountains and hills, may no longer be called to exalt the Lord with us by praise. Their work is to modify all things by blindly starving and murdering everything that is not lucky enough to survive in the universal struggle for hogwash." But this was written very soon after the First World War and in the same decade that brought the Scopes case in this country, in the same general area in which Lincoln had been born in 1809. It was a period in which there was a revival of interest not only in fundamentalist religion but in spiritualism and occultism, which is so often the case after wars.

The issues of the controversy were certainly not as clear-cut as Darwin and the *Origin of Species Through Natural Selection* vs. Butler and Lamarckianism. God and theology were always in the offing. It is a strange triangle—Darwin, Butler, and the Deity. Darwin, who was generally accused of having tried to upset or even put the finishing touches on the fundamental beliefs regarding Divine creation, was always timid about any such assertion. Even at the end of the *Origin of Species,* he was still trying to reconcile his viewpoint with religious attitudes. It is not a very convincing reconciliation, to be sure, but at least an effort. Darwin was definitely against Lamarck and his own grandfather Erasmus Darwin, with their teleological point of view, and against Linnaeus, Cuvier, Agassiz, and others who believed in the special creation of species. With the caginess of the obsessional he could never bring himself to speak against God.[7] Three years before his death he dictated a reply to an inquiry concerning his relation to God:

"Mr Darwin . . . considers that the theory of Evolution is quite compatible with a belief in God; but that you must remember that different persons have different definitions of what they mean by God" (F. Darwin, 1911, 1:277).

[26]

When still in his teens, Darwin had been headed for a career in medicine, largely influenced by his father, and entered the University of Edinburgh where his brother was already a student.[8] While there, even at the age of seventeen, he accomplished a small but creditable piece of research on the movement of the ova of the Flustra, one of the marine corallines, which he reported to the Plinean Society. But he disliked dissecting, and after seeing two operations, one performed on a child without an anaesthetic, he decided to withdraw from medicine and left at the end of his second year.

Next came a move, again paternally propelled, toward Cambridge and preparations to become a clergyman. This seemed to offer a good life for a country gentleman of independent means. But his interests since childhood had been those of a budding naturalist. He devoted his undergraduate time to geology and natural philosophy, and won recognition and friendship from some of his teachers. Then came the chance to go as a naturalist on the world cruise of the *Beagle*. During this period on the *Beagle* (1831-1836) he engaged in the most meticulous observation, collecting and describing an infinite number of specimens of which as many as possible were preserved.

On his return, although not clearly recognized at the time, the direction of his life was determined. The next five years were like an extension of the *Beagle* period in that he continued collecting and studying all kinds of facts which had possible bearing on his emerging theory of the origin of species.[9] This question was very much in the air anyway, and as a young natural philosopher on the brink of studying for the clergy he was peculiarly susceptible to brooding about it. Always a more active investigator than a bookish scholar, he visited farmers, stock breeders, and pigeon fanciers, among others, and read breeders' journals in pursuit of information to correlate with his own observations and surmises, and finally arrived at a firm conviction. This was usually stated with qualifying neurotic caution which may have increased greatly the impression of his modesty.

In 1844 he made a secret draft of his ideas, confiding them only in Professor Lyell[10] at Cambridge and perhaps a few intimates. By this time he had completely given up the idea—which he still had at the beginning of the *Beagle* voyage—that God created the different species. He now thought that they emerged from a few primordial forms. His sense of patricide in entertaining this idea was so great, however, that he wrote to his friend Professor Hooker[11] that in stating his views he felt as though he were confessing murder. It should be noted here that not only God but his father had been opposed to the undertaking of the *Beagle*. This conflict, expressed in obsessional doubts and exaggerated needs for certainty, undoubtedly slowed up his work and made him quite ill. Only in 1859, twenty-three years after his return from the voyage of the *Beagle,* did he publish his theory. Even then it was forced from him by the fact that A. R. Wallace[12] in 1858 came to the very same conclusions that Darwin had been brooding over, and sent a statement of his theory with his notes and observations. To Darwin's horrified amazement, he found almost his own chapter headings in Wallace's papers.

To everyone's credit, no controversy over priority or doubt of Wallace's independent discovery arose. The related charge of plagiarism was to be made later against Darwin by Butler without any reference to Wallace. Professors Lyell and Hooker, who knew well Darwin's priority, agreed that Wallace must be given full recognition for his discovery. Accordingly both men gave papers communicating their findings and theories at the same meeting of the Linnaean Society. Wallace always spoke of Darwin as the master, and Darwin referred to Wallace as the co-discoverer.

To summarize briefly Darwin's theory, which was believed by so many to have abolished God: His argument about the mutability of species began with his collection and observation of a great many specimens showing that offspring tend to vary in many minor ways from their parent stock. The next step was based on the observations of stock breeders that special strains could be developed by propagating together those individuals having similar variations. But, he asked, how was this done in nature? Was there a master mind foreseeing the needs under special conditions, selecting and propagating with these ends in view? This would be only one step removed from divine creation of the species. As early as 1838, the reading of Malthus's *Treatise on Population* served as a catalyst to Darwin's already forming theory—that the extreme fecundity of nature with the ensuing

[29]

struggle for existence served as the great selector. This meant that of the infinite variations in the offspring, only those tended to survive in which the variations were better adapted to local conditions and were produced in sufficient numbers to propagate in a fashion comparable to the artificial selection of breeders. Here there began the harsh rub of the abolition of God, and the substitution of Chance for Divine Plan or Purpose.

The second great heresy lay in the implication that man himself had not been created directly in all his vaunted superiority, but was related to or even descended from the beasts. The *Descent of Man* (1871) left no doubt about this point of view. Certainly the gap between man and his most primitive ancestors (the late frontier of which in the individual lies somewhere on the infant side of the development of secondary-process thinking)—this gap is still generally effective in warding off useful understanding of our bestial selves. Darwin showed extraordinary insight into the importance of the first years in shaping life's patterns.[13] According to him, the first three years were the most important. But he himself was unable to bridge the gap between these years and his later life, just as he could not face how at odds he was with the Creator of his early childhood.

Then he attended a school headed by one of the best classics scholars and most eminent theologians of the day, Dr. Samuel Butler. This Samuel was the grandfather of the Samuel who knew the way of all flesh, but underneath whose crust was so sensitive and

[30]

flinching a fellow that he delayed the publication of his revealing novel almost indefinitely, lest it should hurt the feelings of any of the family whom he pilloried mercilessly in it. Darwin, too, tended to be an appeaser, but in a different way. Although resolutely convinced of the fundamental truth of his theory, when he committed himself to writing he frequently appended a qualifying and almost apologetic note. The haunting question: "How did the primordial forms themselves originate?" got lost in vagueness as belonging to a "period before the first Cambrian Series was deposited," with the implication that this was inevitably a misty time to which one's thoughts could not be expected to penetrate.

When he returned from the voyage of the *Beagle,* he had thought that he was still uncertain whether or not his future path was that of a Church of England clergyman. After 1859, when the theological storm broke around him, he reacted with unusual innocence —something of the quality of innocence which is so characteristic of genius combined with an effective neurotic naïveté. He simply turned away as though he could not possibly understand what people were making a fuss about. He was never openly attacking; never apparently quite recognizing how much his work undermined current religious and biological beliefs.[14] Privately Darwin might write to his friends that he was staggered at the enormously elaborate structure of animal organs, e.g., the eye, the mere contemplation of which tempted him to give credence to the idea that such a design could only arise from

[31]

divinely creative wisdom (F. Darwin, 1911). But tenacious work with a constant testing out of his own ideas seemed always to reinforce his conception that such creative development arose rather from the survival of the fittest, a phrase first used by Herbert Spencer.

Throughout this time Darwin's very severe neurosis was making inroads on his time and energy. There had been some respite and no prolonged relief since his homesickness, his abysmal seasickness, and the severe attacks of malaria while on the voyage of the *Beagle*. By 1840 he seemed to have settled down to chronic nervous and somatic symptoms, and felt that it would take him many years to recover. His illness, not unlike Spencer's and that of many other Victorians, threatened his working life and subsequently banished him for periods of residence in hydrotherapeutic and other sanatoria for weeks together.

He had married in 1839, and was expecting his first child by the end of the year. In August, however, he was writing in his diary that he was "much unwell and scandalously idle." He moralized that he had derived at least this much good from his enforced rest, that he now realized that *nothing* was so intolerable as idleness. His notes refer chiefly to being "unwell," to "being completely knocked up" and having cardiac palpitations after correcting proofs; to the dread of going out; and at times to the dread of "hereditary ill-health." At thirty-one (1840), he wrote that he had become a "dull, old spiritless dog. . . . One gets stupider as one gets older, I think"; and at forty-nine, in a letter to his friend Professor Hooker, he referred to himself as "your insane and perverse friend," perhaps because the enjoyment of specimens he had received did not come up at all to his anticipations. One recognizes a certain quiet drama in his complaints, but no doubt he suffered greatly. His symptoms were those which fifty years ago would have been called neurasthenia. Probably now we would think of them as a severe anxiety neurosis in an obsessional character, certainly much complicated by genius. Perhaps we would not even venture a diagnosis in a condition with such polymorphous symptomatology.

In 1860 he was writing to Asa Gray, his American friend at Harvard, that the theological view of the question of Evolution was exceedingly painful and bewildering to him, and protested that he had no intention of writing atheistically. Although his health was so bad that he hardly passed a day without distress, he saw no connection between his nervousness and his inner spiritual and personal struggle; only that his work got larger and larger and threatened to sweep him away. When at the age of sixty-four he was torn between considering that a beneficent God would not permit the immense misery in the world, and opposite thoughts of a grand and wondrous universe which seemed the chief argument for the existence of God, he retreated to the safe conclusion that the whole subject (of God) is beyond man's intellect, adding hopefully that man, however, could do his duty. There is some indication that this struggle lasted up to the very end of his life. This is regarded by some as an indication of weakness in Darwin's belief in his own findings and theories. It seems more likely evidence of the severity of his neurosis, in which conviction of his own worth and fear of his father came into conflict.

Certain qualities of Darwin's character must be considered in any understanding of the greatness of his accomplishments and limitations imposed on his actual work. First of all he was a gentleman rather than a scholar. In his youth he seemed headed toward becoming a country gentleman, a horseman, a hunter, and even something of a gay blade, to an extent that worried his father, the affluent, energetic Dr. Robert Waring Darwin, leading physician of Shrewsbury. Charles Darwin was not an exhaustive reader, and did not always know thoroughly and in detail all of the work which preceded his own. This was apparent in the contrast between him and the intellectually exuberant Thomas Huxley who became his watchdog. A field worker and, to a degree, an experimenter, he was possessed of the need for careful, assiduously thorough observation. But he was not a literary man; nor did he always know well all of the technical literature of his chosen field. But undoubtedly he had the vision and the fresh innocence of mind of the genius: what has been called the ability to make the lucky guess and then prove it with facts. We would think of this gift rather as the ability to form preconscious Gestalt observations which jostle each other for survival of the fittest as they coalesce into new patterns in a way to be compared with Darwin's own theory,

[34]

until the likeliest ones spring forth into consciousness, seemingly as guesses or inspirations.

The slow growth of Darwin's neurosis, however, made constrictions. He retired into vagueness at certain crucial points in a way typical of the obsessional. He progressively lost contact with life outside his family and his chosen field. His interest in poetry, music, and the landscape, which in his boyhood had comforted and delighted him, became atrophied or lost. Even in his work he felt encroachments. Toward the end of his life, when he frequently feared loss of memory, he also complained: "my mind seems to have become a machine for grinding general laws out of collections of facts" (Barlow, 1958).

It is not surprising to learn, then, how almost casual sometimes Darwin's interest appeared even in regard to his immediate predecessors, including his own grandfather, Erasmus Darwin. He attacked them, to be sure. But his was not always a highly specific and critical examination of their writing, but rather an all-out effort to show with the burden of all the facts which he had mustered that his theory was right and theirs must be correspondingly wrong. In his *Autobiography* he described himself as "not very sceptical." He denied that he owed anything at all in his scientific viewpoint to the work of Erasmus, saying this in response to a reproach from Samuel Butler.

In his failure to pay the fullest attention to his scientific rivals he again showed the limitations of the obsessional person who avoids paralyzing doubts by concentrating on a central arena of endeavor, although this was always threatening to get out of control and drown him in a sea of details. In the less gifted this kind of concentration often leads to tubular vision and to rigid or fanatical dogmatism. Coupled with genius, it permitted an intensity of devotion expressed in perfectionism which was extraordinarily fruitful. The direct, harsh, compelling competitiveness which is so often the burden of neurotic perfectionism was seemingly absent. This may have been due to his intrinsic genius, but also was part of his habitual but mild ignoring of rivals, although he treated them with exquisitely patient personal courtesy if they wrote him or intruded into his life. Privately he might let himself go to the extent of writing to an intimate friend: "Heaven forfend me from Lamarck's nonsense . . . and veritable rubbish." His grandfather, Erasmus, probably had a place in this cloud of contempt. There is little doubt, however, but that he would have been friendly and quietly charming to Lamarck or to Erasmus Darwin if he had met them in person. He was somewhat shy of robust characters like Erasmus unless they had already shown themselves to be on his side. His capacity for detachment protected him. His was a vague, passive, but drastic elimination which he himself seemed to recognize metaphorically as murder.

Darwin's early intensively competitive ambition is clearly indicated in some of his letters. But the very intensity of this caused it to be repressed, and contributed to his neurosis—by which, however, he could salvage something in a purified form at the expense of the dangerous neurotic mechanism of denial. Darwin's description of his ambition was as follows: "Sedgwick called my father and said I should take a place among the leading scientific men. . . . After reading this letter, I clambered over the mountains of Ascension with a bounding step and made the volcanic rocks resound under my geological hammer; but I think I can say with truth that in after years, though I cared in the highest degree for approbation of such men as Lyell and Hooker, who were my friends, I did not care much about the general public." This was in the Cambridge period.

After there had been an increase in his neurotic symptoms in 1840, he wrote: "My father scarcely seems to expect that I shall become strong for some years; it has been a bitter mortification for me to digest the conclusion that 'the race is for the strong' and that I shall probably do little more but be content to admire the strides that others make in Science."

Late in 1859, the year of the publication of the *Origin of Species,* young Samuel Butler left England for New Zealand. At the same time he ceased his life-long habit of saying of his prayers. The son of a canon and the grandson of a bishop, he had just renounced the prospect of ordination to find his fortune as a sheep farmer, and prepare to become a painter. His father had refused his blessing and his financial support even more emphatically than had Charles Darwin's father a generation before, when Charles had gone on the *Beagle.* Both fathers feared their sons might get into bad company and would have preferred to see them safely ordained in the Church of England, where with the backing of adequate family fortunes and connections they could lead comfortable, gentlemanly lives, continuing classical studies or conducting botanical experiments as a hobby.

During the first year and a half, Butler established himself on a sheep farm of 8,000 acres, which he named Mesopotamia because it was between two rivers. He continued his study of the New Testament, and found himself increasingly able to form his own independent opinions. Presently he was writing to a college friend that he could no longer believe that Christ had died on the cross, and further that he could not make head or tail of the Trinity; he had renounced Christianity altogether, and had discontinued attendance at church. This had not made the least change in his digestion. Like Charles Darwin at the same age, he felt no need to earn money when there was a sufficient family fortune at hand, and he resented his father's lack of compliant generosity. His letters to his father were as acrimonious and raspingly direct in his statements of his needs as Darwin's had been apologetic, explanatory, and indirect in the days of the *Beagle*. Canon Butler did not trust his son's practical judgment, and the relationship between them became increasingly unpleasant and grating.

Probably in 1861 or early 1862, Butler read Darwin's *Origin of Species* and was immediately enthralled. Soon he was writing a "Dialogue on Darwinism" for the Christchurch *Press*. (Christchurch here is the name of a nearby town.) This article elicited a counterattack from the Bishop of Wellington, and still later (1863) brought him a letter from Darwin himself, endorsing Butler's clear statement of his ideas. Nevertheless the very dialectical form of his presentation forecast the fundamental ambivalence of Butler's attitude toward all fathers, whether in the Church, in science, or in classical studies. Already in 1863 his readiness to attack Darwin was emerging, although he himself seemed unaware of it. He wrote then a satirical article "Darwin Among the Machines." His thesis, which he seemed to regard as a bit of playfulness but which was taken quite seriously by many readers, was that all advanced machines should be destroyed lest through continued evolution they gain the upper hand over man. This article and another, "Lucubratio Ebria," published in 1865 after his return to England, formed the nuclei for later expansions in *Erewhon* and *Life and Habit*. The ideas expressed formed the core of his later repeated attacks on Darwin's theories. At the same time he was publishing anonymously a pamphlet presenting a critical examination of the evidence of the resurrection of Jesus Christ. Evidently he was not as free from his religious preoccupations and concerns as he thought.

Butler got on well enough in New Zealand; he made a small nest egg and some friendships. It is an appealing picture: this young expatriate in his sheep farmer's shack, back of the beyond yet housing his piano brought by bullock dray, and his books which he considered more than anything else to represent him truly. He was astute enough to realize that changing conditions in New Zealand probably limited his prospects. Consequently he sold out when he could still realize a profit. Besides he was homesick for intellectual contacts, although he had made out quite well in the rougher New Zealand life and was never patronizing in his attitude toward its people.

He was disappointed that his pamphlet disproving the resurrection of Christ made no great stir in England.[15] He sent a copy to Darwin, who was impressed with it and wrote him cordially. In reply Butler opened his heart to Darwin to the extent of confiding in writing about his past plans and present determination to become a painter. He flattered the older man, expressing his delight in the *Origin of Species,* and perhaps overemphasizing his humility beside Darwin. Although Butler thought himself to have become independent of concern about other people's opinions, it seems clear that no man longed more to have his opinions at least a matter of controversy. He could hardly help but be jealous of Darwin, who was the center of so much stir and seemed to make so little of it. But at this time Butler was much identified with Darwin, ready to accept him as a kind of spiritual father and realize some gratification through him.

Butler's grandfather and Darwin's father had been two of the three leading men in Shrewsbury. Darwin had gone to school to the elder Samuel Butler (later Bishop), and had been a contemporary at Cambridge of Butler's father, Tom Butler. The younger Samuel Butler was also on friendly terms with Darwin's son, Francis. During the decade from 1865 to 1875, Butler continued to write Darwin, sent him books, and twice in 1872 visited him at Down House. Some have thought that Butler was miffed at not being received in a more wholehearted fashion; and certainly no deep intimacy developed. From his letters it seems that Butler was somewhat in awe of Darwin, unaware of his disappointment or of his growing hostility. He was rather sadly anxious to have Darwin's approval, and ready to doubt himself in the underlying anti-Darwin ideas which gradually grew in his mind.

During the early part of this period he was still hoping to become a great painter, and was spending a great deal of time at Heatherley's Art School, with marginal efforts to convert fellow students to Darwinism. The *Origin of Species* had become his Bible. He continued to be preoccupied with the question of whether or not Christ survived the crucifixion, and seemed unable to settle this for himself. It seemed to him the greatest irony, a kind of theological practical joke or hoax, that perhaps Christ had not died on the cross at all. The question of the postcrucifixion survival of Christ became the subject of his book *The Fair Haven* (1873).

As Butler's interest in evolution developed and got beyond the stage of his pleasure in its use as a weapon against his father's religion, he still needed to find a spiritual content to science and a scientific basis for religion. Rather subtly he became dissatisfied with Darwin's views, which seemed to leave too much to chance. He could not see the universe without an all-encompassing design. He was, however, no biologist, either by temperament or training. He lived in meager quarters in London, with the merest courtyard for an out-of-doors. On his summer excursions, mostly on the Continent, he was interested in sketching, art, in visiting museums, and churches, in people, and he showed a keen responsiveness to Nature. But there was not the interest of a scientist in the least. His biologizing was part, rather, of his constant philosophical contemplation and reading, with some self-harassment since it took him away from his painting and his music. He was thus in great contrast to Darwin, who was above all a direct and persistent observer, fitting pieces of the puzzle together with endless patience and enduring interest.

Things began to come to a head when late in 1877 Butler discovered that his own book *Life and Habit,* just published,[16] was more of an attack on Darwinism than he had realized. It was really his own adaptation of Lamarckianism, with an extension into the realms of the spirit and the psyche. He saw evolution as coming about through the tendency of each biological organism to register every bit of its experience in the modifications of its structure and functioning. He conceived of this gradually changing structure as being an organic memory record, permanently built in, like organic habits, and reproduced in the offspring. Its operation on an organic basis might be compared very roughly with ideas of unconscious mental functioning, which had already been glimpsed but did not come into any usable theoretical form until Freud.

Life and Habit was illuminated by smart epigrammatic statements slightly suggestive of Wilde or of Shaw. "Birth," said Butler, "has been made too much of . . . it has often been remarked that a hen is only an egg's way of making another egg." As his friend and biographer H. Festing Jones (1919) later reported, "Butler's whole nature revolted against the idea of a universe without intelligence. . . . He could not return to the Jewish and Christian idea of God designing his creatures from outside; he saw, however, no reason why the intelligence should not be inside." He adopted the Lamarckian idea of the organism's sense of need in its response to the environment, and referred to it rather as "faith and desire, aided by intelligence." He was a bit boastful about his ignorance of science, writing: "I know nothing about science, and it is well that there should be no mistake on this head. I neither know nor want to know more detail than is necessary to enable me to give a fairly broad and comprehensive view of the subject."

He was very excited in the writing of *Life and Habit,* alternating a high pitch of conviction with morbidly insistent doubt, and is reported to have been unable to breathe quite properly for a whole year after he finished it. His symptoms in this period certainly somewhat resembled Darwin's. But his were acute, whereas Darwin's were chronic. He considered the book his masterpiece which was to shake the world, even as Darwin's *Origin of Species* had already done. It was also to recoup his fortunes, which had been sorely depleted by poor investments. At this point his inner conflict about Darwin definitely emerged. He sent two copies of the book to Francis Darwin with a painfully frank letter in which he stated his position. One copy was intended for Charles Darwin if Francis should "think fit after reading it." He felt that he neither intended nor wished to attack Darwin, but was simply driven into it by the need for the Truth. He concluded his letter with special regrets that he must make an attack on one who had been at school under his grandfather.

Darwin ignored the book. Other biologists regarded it as a huge joke. Somewhat similar ideas had been presented by the physiologist, Hering,[17] some seven or eight years earlier, and had at least won some dignified notice. It is probable that Butler's literary presentation, proudly lacking documentation or evidence of direct experience, contributed to his painful position. Even before this, he had had a way of externalizing his controversies in forms that just did not catch on. His publications seemed generally to flop, and he made no money on any of them. It was the same story with *Life and Habit* (1877) as it had been with the pamphlet on the *Resurrection of Jesus Christ* (1865b). In both instances, too, someone else's earlier presentation containing views similar to his had gained some recognition. This same year of 1877 marked the renunciation of his ambition to be a painter. In his own words, his "career as an art student just fizzled out." From then on he substituted the Reading Room of the British Museum for the studio.

In 1879, he published *Evolution Old and New,* comparing the theories of Buffon, Erasmus Darwin, and Lamarck with those of Charles Darwin. He was certainly after Darwin now, marshaling Darwin's own grandfather on his side and claiming that Charles Darwin had taken ideas from Erasmus without giving credit. This book was followed soon by *Unconscious Memory* (1880). Butler's vision had reached such dimensions that he was planning a book which would show that "every molecule is full of will and consciousness; the motion of the stars in Space is voluntary and of a design on their part." He planned to give a quotation from Walt Whitman on the title page.

The controversy now began to take the form of a bitter personal quarrel, at least on Butler's side. It was to leave a persistently festering wound for the rest of his life. In a way quite typical of him, Darwin refused to quarrel, and scarcely answered back, but went his own way repeating his own views. Darwin was now at the height of his reputation, and commanded something like the reverence or awe which Butler had once felt, but awareness of which must now have been grueling to him who could not even elicit anger. Butler extended the allegation of a kind of plagiarism on Darwin's part from his grandfather, Erasmus, to a further charge that Darwin had allowed quotations from Butler himself to be used in a book on Erasmus Darwin without acknowledging their source. There was a nucleus of truth in Butler's charges, but the situation was not of great moment and had not developed as part of deliberately evil intentions on Darwin's side; rather it had been a combination of probably unavoidable error and some neurotically determined oversights. Butler clearly found a toehold for his increasing hostility to Darwin, and made the most of it until it developed into a paranoid attitude which he was never able to overcome. The actual events of the misunderstanding (which might have been clarified if Darwin had been more directly outspoken) were never made clear to both sides of the controversy until 1911, years after the deaths of both Darwin and Butler. Then H. Festing Jones and Francis Darwin came together, compared documents, and published the facts.

This unpleasant situation had arisen in connection with the translation of a sketch of the life of Erasmus Darwin by Ernst Krause, in February, 1879. This was first entitled "A Contribution to the History of the Descent-Theory" and appeared as an article in the German scientific journal *Kosmos,* about two months before the publication of Butler's *Evolution Old and New,* in which he took up the cudgels for Erasmus and against Charles Darwin. The latter agreed to a translation of the Krause sketch and wrote a preface in which he endorsed it in a statement that the translator's scientific reputation and his knowledge of German furnished a guarantee for its accuracy. It appeared in England as a small book entitled the *Life of Erasmus Darwin* in November, 1879. On reading the translation Butler detected passages which were drawn from his book *Evolution Old and New,* which had appeared in May, 1879 (i.e., after the German sketch in *Kosmos* but before the English translation). These passages were not only not acknowledged as coming from him, but were used against his point of view. Thus he was doubly hurt. Since they were seemingly endorsed by Charles Darwin, Butler felt that the situation was less than straightforward. Darwin's answer acknowledged that additions to the original text *had* been made, but disclaimed any intentions such as Butler attributed to him. He offered to make a correction in any future editions of the book, and sent Butler the reference to the original article. But he did not acknowledge himself as a criminal, and he did not satisfy the enraged Butler. The disagreement went the way such affairs often do, and was next brought out to the public in the pages of the Athenaeum as well as furnishing fuel for Butler's book on *Unconscious Memory.*

Butler had now deserted painting altogether, and was writing furiously and publishing quickly, though at his own expense. Actually the additions had been made by Krause, to whom Darwin had sent a copy of Butler's *Life and Habit,* since it contained references to Erasmus Darwin. Charles Darwin's generally meticulous care had understandably enough fallen down in the editing of the final form of the book, and he had inadvertently vouched for its complete accuracy. Darwin's neurosis was possibly at work here, for he had to a degree repudiated the work of Erasmus, whom he considered an unreliable speculator. He had done here what he did on some other occasions of conflict, viz., taken leave of his usual caution and looked the other way.

But Butler's attack came like a small-sized and bewildering hurricane. Darwin, an old man and famous, seemed at first paralyzed and then went into an obsessional frenzy of indecision about what he should do, invoking a family council to advise him. When this did not work, he called on Leslie Stephen and Thomas Huxley, who advised ignoring Butler and remaining silent. This was not perhaps the best advice, for it did not help to bring out the facts, and Butler was not a man to take the silent treatment well. The whole matter rankled with him insistently, and in his bitterness he probably damaged his own reputation further. This in brief was the story of the Darwin-Butler controversy.

Certain attitudes of Darwin's contributed indirectly to the feelings in Butler which touched off the controversy. First among these was his position in regard to speculation, and second was his estimate of his grandfather, Erasmus Darwin. Charles was exceedingly, even neurotically, intolerant of speculation. Even the slightest flight of creative fantasy was suspect, and he could commit nothing to print without the extremest preliminary efforts at validation. The roots of this strong reaction formation lay in his childhood. Late in life he was forced to admit that without some capacity for speculative thought there could be no development of scientific theory, and no formulation of scientific problems. But he arrived at this only after a struggle.

Further, Darwin could not openly and publicly express hostility. Even when he expressed hostile attitudes or criticisms in his letters to his friends, such remarks were often couched in colloquial terms as though to make a slight joke of it all. This of course was the exact antithesis of the behavior of Butler, whose anger seemed to enhance his drive toward productivity, though it might vitiate the content of what he wrote. He privately went out of his way to be kind and thoughtful, especially to those under him, but his gift of slashing satire came to the fore in most of his writing. Darwin's hostility emerged in ways unknown to himself, first in his persistent neurotic mechanism of denial with quick and sweeping forgetting or ignoring of work which he did not value; and second, less decisively, in his vagueness when he was brought into personal contact with the authors of such work. Although the surface was generally calm and winning, except for the invasion of somatic manifestations of his neurosis, privately he was thrown readily into morbid doubt, guilt feelings, and indecision.

When Darwin, with the reinforcement of Leslie Stephen and Thomas Huxley, ignored Butler's charges, the latter announced that Darwin had not defended himself because he had no defense. How much Darwin suffered is evident in his letter of acknowledgment to Huxley: "I feel like a man condemned to be hanged who has been granted a reprieve. I saw in the future no end of trouble, but I feared that I was bound in honour to answer. . . . The affair has annoyed me and pained me to a silly extent."

This predisposition to the feelings of anxiety and

guilt was manifest in many forms and situations, and increased his demand for compulsive accuracy and his periodic befuddling doubt. It may be one reason why his enthusiasm never appeared as a full inspirational state. His general enjoyment became more limited, his aesthetic responsiveness chained, and even his personal relationships limited as the years wore on. It was while describing his inability to be convinced of the existence of God that he wrote in his *Autobiography:* "In my Journal [i.e., at twenty-three or so] I wrote that while standing in the midst of the grandeur of the Brazilian forest it is not possible to give an adequate idea of the higher feelings of wonder, admiration and devotion which fill and elevate the mind; but now the grandest scenes would not cause any such convictions and feelings to rise in my mind. It may be truly said that I am like a man who has become colour-blind, and the universal belief by man of the existence of redness makes my present loss of perception of not the least value as evidence. . . . The state of mind which grand scenes formerly excited in me and which was intimately connected with a belief in God, did not essentially differ from that which is often called the sense of sublimity; and however difficult it may be to explain the genesis of this sense, it can hardly be advanced as an argument for the existence of God, any more than the powerful though vague and similar feelings excited by music." (Surely this reminds us of the conversation between Freud and Romain Rolland.)

That he had originally been tempted to wild flights

of fantasy is apparent, not only from the limited anecdotes of his childhood, but from the thickness of the
barrier of abhorrence which he created against the
evil of speculation. Erasmus Darwin, the grandfather
and sinful speculator whom Charles did not know,
since he died seven years before Charles was born,
was a man fertile and active in mind and body. Unlike Charles he disliked field sports and hunting, but
otherwise spread his activities widely—writing poetry,
making crude mechanical and electrical experiments
and inventions, and late in life publishing a number
of pamphlets including an extensive treatise: *A Con-
cise and Easy Introduction to the Sexual Botany of
Linnaeus.* He was active, enthusiastic, and experi-
mental in the practice of medicine from which he
gained renown and prosperity. Well known for his
vivid and extravagant imagination and art, he was the
sort of man about whom colorful anecdotes naturally
grow. Certainly he was not in the least afraid of fanci-
ful ideas or behavior. No full-length biography of him
has ever been written, only a brief, gossipy one by a
contemporary lady writer (Anna Seward, 1804; see
also Ashmun, 1931), and the even briefer sketch by
Krause (1879), the translation of which unwittingly
precipitated the Darwin-Butler controversy. This was
the grandfather, then, whose influence on him Charles
Darwin was to dismiss after a second reading of the
Zoonomia (1744), because of "the proportion of speculation being so large to the facts given." In defense
of Charles Darwin's disclaimer of Erasmus's positive
influence, it is noteworthy that Samuel Taylor Cole-

[51]

ridge, who in his youth had been impressed by Erasmus Darwin's scientific and literary productions, later felt a revulsion from their crudity and inexactness. He coined the word Darwinizing for wildly speculative hypothesizing. In Charles's youth the word may have become a cant term with this meaning.

But it is also possible that Charles Darwin displaced onto Erasmus, whom he did not know, some of the hostility for his own father, which had to remain unconscious. Some yearning really to have known this dynamic and robust grandfather came through in Charles when, as a man of sixty-seven, he began work on his own autobiography, and wrote in its opening paragraph: "I have thought that the attempt [to write an autobiographical sketch] would amuse me and might possibly interest my children or their children. I know that it would have interested me greatly to have read even so short and dull a sketch of the mind of my grandfather written by himself, and what he thought and did and how he worked. I have attempted to write the following account of myself as if I were a dead man in another world looking back at my life."

Samuel Butler had a grandfather, too, whose namesake he was—and who died almost on his fourth birthday. He appears only very vaguely as a man of God, a bishop, of greater importance and reputation than Butler's own father, but with no direct or specific influence in the controversy. Discussion of his role in the lives of the two men is left for the next, the biographical chapter.

The Biographical Background
of the Controversialists

IT IS ALREADY clear that the controversy was not
merely a conflict of ideas, but rather that it involved
a change in the emotional axis of the relationship
between the two men which had occurred very gradually. The ideas which seemed so concerned with the
philosophic and scientific truth, especially on Butler's
side, had become the vehicles for emotional attitudes
highly personal in origin, of which the adversaries
were dimly, if at all, aware. Before coming to a further
examination of the interlacing patterns of the quest
for the father as it appeared in direct and reversed
form in these two men, we must look further at their
life conflicts and problems.

Although Charles Darwin was not an introspective
man, he probably wanted passionately to understand
those around him and himself. But this had to come
to him through careful observation of the minutest
details of the behavior of others. Although he was
intensely concerned with the study of the expression
of emotion in man and animals, his autobiography
gives the impression of a considerable muting of ex-

pression of his own emotions. He could be kindly and sympathetic, and one gets no sense of falseness about it, but there is a general vagueness which is hard to describe. Such a state probably came as a reaction formation against critical disturbances of childhood, with the subsequent need to repress all strong emotion because of the danger of being overwhelmed or driven into unacceptable action by it. It *may* also have been reinforced by an ambivalent identification with his extremely well-ordered and repressed father, Dr. Robert Waring Darwin.[18]

This father, having resented being forced to study medicine by *his* father, the exuberant Erasmus, still became a successful and fashionable practitioner, unusually able to win confidence by his unfailing cheerfulness. He was a man of impressive size. He hated his profession, sickened at the thought of an operation, and could not endure the sight of blood. He practiced mostly a kind of marriage-counseling psychotherapy, realizing that more of his patients were sick from unhappy marriages than from physical diseases. He seemed particularly able to detect the dire and hidden distresses in others, and he made quite a reputation for being able to read character when he distrusted at sight a newcomer in town who soon turned out to be a swindler. His young son Charles gained the impression that his father could tell *his* innermost thoughts. After his wife's death when he was fifty-one, he did not marry again, and whatever amours he may have had were well concealed. He had named his two sons for his unfortunate brothers:

Charles who died from an infection contracted during dissecting work as a medical student, and Erasmus who committed suicide by drowning during a fit of melancholia. In spite of his dislike of his profession, he insisted that both his sons should study medicine, but he could not force them to become practitioners. That the doctor possessed a durable façade of compulsive enthusiasm was tacitly admitted by his children, who referred to his arrival home each afternoon as the incoming of the Tide.[19] This meant that all must be silent while he held the center of the stage.

Charles Darwin in childhood may have confused God and his father, who was over six feet tall and weighed 340 pounds. He seemed never to overcome or really admit his fear of this colossal parent. The very superlatives of admiration and dutiful respect with which Charles habitually spoke of his father betrayed the unadmitted conflict in regard to him. Yet they had some happy times together, especially when the father took Charles on rounds with him. Together they would enjoy the beauty of the countryside and share some interest in flowers. Some years after his father's death, Charles, accompanied by his own children, visited again the Shrewsbury home of his childhood and tried in vain to recapture the memory of his father there. The difficulty was attributed by him to the intrusions of having others around him.

Robert Darwin did not consider his son Charles especially bright, but rather a little below the average in intelligence and certainly not as bright as the sister one year younger, with whom he was constantly paired. After quoting his father as having said to him: "You care for nothing but shooting, dogs, and rat-catching, and you will be a disgrace to yourself and all your family," Charles typically adds: "But my father, who was the kindest man I ever knew, and whose memory I love with all my heart, must have been angry and somewhat unjust when he used these words" (Barlow, 1958, p. 22). Such was his bondage of duty and respect still at the age of sixty-seven.

Charles's mother was ailing in his infancy, and died after a long invalidism when he was eight. He was then cared for by his sister, nine years older, who was so zealous in her efforts to improve him that for years afterward he could scarcely enter a door without thinking: "What will she blame me for now?" He became "dogged" so as not to care too much whatever she said. This capacity for protective abstraction lasted throughout his life, but kept him from a deeper understanding of himself and of others. But this gifted child turned his attention elsewhere. He looked, listened, and observed; became a collector of all kinds of objects: shells, seals, coins, and beetles, with a real and lasting passion. He was the only one of the six children of the family who developed so special an interest.[20] This led him to believe that it was innate. In some degree he may have been correct—to the extent that he was the only one possessed of an inherent gift which asserted itself in spite of the considerable odds against the development of individuality in this motherless family. They did not seem to be an unhappy family, certainly, though weighed down by their portentous father who knew without question what was the best for everyone.

Charles built up not only doggedness but other reaction formations against any show of anger or aggression. He became aware of his appetite for power, revealed early in an incident of beating a puppy; and he developed then a particularly severe conscience demanding always gentleness and patience of himself, with morbid indecision and self-doubting when called upon for the least show of even reasonable aggression. It is probable that his periodic physical misery, the description of which sounds so much like primitive anxiety, arose in response to such needs. He had managed by passive resistance to extricate himself from the study of medicine after two years in Edinburgh. Later to make decisions and to publish articles were already acts of aggression against God and his father, as a show of independence and a disavowal of his father's all-seeing authority. Only in hunting did he allow his sadistic sporting pleasure a place. This had begun at fifteen in response to a taunt from his stepuncle, Samuel Galton, who told him that the birds sat in the trees and laughed at him. After this he was determined to become a good marksman, and succeeded (Barlow, 1958).

His insomnia, too, was sometimes in response to fear of his own aggression, as is clearly indicated in several anecdotes told in his *Life and Letters*. For example, in 1865 Edward Eyre, Governor of Jamaica, suppressed a Negro uprising with considerable brutality. The following year, when he was being tried for murder, English public opinion formed two camps. Darwin felt the prosecution was correct, but in a controversial discussion with one of his sons he "spoke almost with fury." Subsequently he could not sleep, and appeared at the young man's bedside early in the morning asking for forgiveness.[21] It may be significant that only a few months earlier, Fitzroy (who had been Captain of the *Beagle*, and with whom Darwin had had great though quiet difficulty) had committed suicide. This act in itself could not but have stirred Charles profoundly. The obsessional need for accuracy was also strengthened by his fear of making an exaggerated statement while angry. On one occasion he went in the night to the house of a nearby clergyman to set the score straight after a debate at a parish meeting. Darwin's statement had been technically accurate, and the subject was of no great moment. But he could not sleep with the thought that he might have been misunderstood.[22] While at Cambridge he could still show active justified temper without great alarm. At that time he was described as a lively young man overflowing with animal spirits. On one occasion he denounced a fellow student and threatened to kick him downstairs when he caught the fellow pilfering from his beetle collection.[23] His neurotic fear of killing seemed to progress greatly, dating from the period on the *Beagle*, and it carried with it the complementary fear of dying himself.

Charles probably suffered early from severe confusion of sexual orientation—an understandable state of affairs with a sister barely a year younger. This confusion is obvious in a screen memory from the age of four: he was sitting on his sister Caroline's knee (she was thirteen and probably maturing) when he was so startled by seeing a cow run past the window that he jumped up and cut himself on a knife which she was using to peel an orange. In another memory from the same time, it was not clear whether it was he or the younger sister Catherine who had been shut up in a room for punishment. He was considered a difficult child, given to fabrications, daydreaming, solitary walks about which he told marvelous stories. He was gullible, and believed in magic at a time when most children are wiser.

He was early interested in flowers, and recalled having told a young schoolmate that he could change the color of polyanthuses and primroses by watering them with different colored fluids. The comrade remembered further that Charles had brought a flower to school and shown how his mother had taught him that by looking at the inside of the blossom the name of the plant could be discovered. It is likely that both of these memories are screens, and that young Charles and his friend were preoccupied with questions about the anatomical sexual differences and whether urine possessed magic qualities. The incidents occurred rather soon after Charles's mother's death.[24]

Her death produced the first massive denial in the child. He later thought of her as having died in his infancy, even though he knew otherwise. He could never remember her—only her black velvet gown and her rather curiously constructed worktable. About the same time he witnessed the burial of a dragoon and remembered chiefly the man's empty boots and his carbine hanging from his saddle. Thus there was a displacement from the body to its accoutrements, certainly an indication of conflict and distress. But the detailed content and accompanying fantasies are not known.[25] It may be that the mysteries of both sex and death, however much denied in the personal experience, increased this gifted child's ponderings and contributed to his scientific investigativeness.[26] One suspects that his turn to science, and especially the empirical elements in it, was derived also from facets of his ambivalent identification with his father and his grandfather, but even more from reactions to sadomasochistic fantasies concerning his own birth and his mother's death. In his autobiography the almost empty areola of memory surrounding her death remains as a negative monument, for he did not mention her again. She was Susannah Wedgwood, the daughter of Josiah, famous Staffordshire potter who was a close friend of his grandfather, Erasmus Darwin. She was one year older than his father. When Charles came to marriage at thirty, he chose his cousin Emma Wedgwood, also one year older than himself, and the daughter of another Josiah Wedgwood. In this way, perhaps, some memory was expressed. If so, it was of the kind about which Samuel Butler (1880) quipped in saying: "We remember our past experiences, though too utterly to be capable of introspection in the matter."

But some years before his marriage, a considerable

change had come into his life. He had left medicine at Edinburgh and certainly was vague about his theological expectations at Cambridge. He settled so readily into the study of natural history and his ability attracted enough attention that he came to realize his own superiority. This period seemed indeed a turning point in his life, and probably never again did he fundamentally distrust his own ability, although he might get into states of morbid doubt about various stages of his progress. Consciously he took the praise somewhat uneasily, and still considered himself as committed to becoming a clergyman —ultimately. There was no great dedication in the expectation, however. Clearly he was in love with science, with geology in the central position. It was Henslow,[27] professor of geology, who recommended him for the position of naturalist on the *Beagle,* and supported him even in the face of his father's devaluation and opposition.[28] But it was his Uncle Josiah Wedgwood (Emma's father) who finally intervened and won his father over, in spite of Charles's recent sins of overspending his allowance while at Cambridge. With the sailing of the *Beagle* at Christmas 1831, he was definitely conscious that a new life was beginning, and likened it to a rebirth.

But it was also associated with the overt development of his very considerable neurosis.[29] Captain Fitzroy, who commanded the *Beagle,* was only a few years older than Charles, i.e., just the age of the brother Erasmus.[30] For whatever reasons, he is repeatedly referred to in the *Autobiography* and the

Notes as only a year older, which would put him in the same chronological relationship to Charles that Charles had to his sister Catherine. Charles took to him immediately: thought him direct, energetic, and ardent as well as unusually handsome, and believed that he resembled King Charles II. But the Captain, who was an earnest follower of the Swiss mystic physiognomist Lavater, had a considerable antipathy to the shape of young Darwin's nose, and would have disqualified him at once if there had been another likely candidate for the position. The two men had to share the cramped quarters of the captain's cabin.

Fitzroy was not only extraordinarily courageous; he was conscientious and idealistic to the point of moral sadism. He was a Tory, strongly class-conscious, a believer in harsh discipline both for himself and his men, and a righteous supporter of slavery. Yet he struggled to be absolutely just and fair, at the expense of increasing tension. For a time he was subject to almost daily rages, referred to euphemistically by the junior officers as "serving out hot coffee," and he had occasional fits of black melancholy. At one time Fitzroy had gone through a period of religious doubt. Having re-established his belief with a degree of fanaticism, he apparently disapproved of the trend of Darwin's interests. Charles was impressed with the Captain's ability to hold an ascendancy over others, and could even imagine him as a Nelson or a Napoleon, but did not consider him really clever. Charles is reputed never to have lost his temper, and was nicknamed the *Philosopher* or the *Flycatcher,* just as at the Shrewsbury school he had been called *Gas* because of his chemical experiments. He was naturally always afraid of precipitating a rage in the Captain.

Palpitations with fear of heart trouble which had beset him even before he boarded the *Beagle* gave way to bouts of the extremest seasickness and all manner of gastrointestinal disturbances. In spite of this he was able to do a fantastic amount of work, some of which required great physical endurance. He was never again free from symptoms, however, for more than a few weeks at a time.

As for Fitzroy, his quixotic career continued. In 1845 he made something of a fiasco of his governorship of New Zealand when he antagonized fellow Tories by championing the rights of natives against unscrupulous white settlers. Following this he won some distinction when he commanded one of the new screw frigates and became an admiral, Fellow of the Royal Society, and in 1854 chief of the department of meteorology of the Board of Trade. He is credited with having established the system of storm warnings which preceded weather reporting. The full force of Fitzroy's hostility to Darwin came into the open in 1860, when at a stormy meeting of the British Association at Oxford in which the theory of evolution by natural selection was debated and the facts questioned, Fitzroy arose, waving a Bible aloft, and calling on it as a witness, denied Huxley's statements of the factual basis of the theory, cited how often he had protested to his former shipmate because of the latter's irreligious views, and regretted that the *Origin*

[63]

of Species had ever been published. At this same meeting Bishop Samuel Wilberforce asked Huxley whether it was through grandfather or grandmother that he claimed descent from a monkey, and Huxley replied that he would rather have an ape for an ancestor than an intellectual prostitute like Wilberforce. After his outbreak Fitzroy continued tense, irritable, and explosive, but probably had no direct contact with Darwin. In 1865 he slashed his own throat in a state of melancholic anger. The effect of this on Darwin is not clear.

Charles Darwin married Emma Wedgwood about three years after the return of the *Beagle*. Beside the flashes of passionate joy in his scientific pursuits, the personal attachment seemed to take second place. Some time in 1837 or 1838, thinking of marriage obsessionally and in the abstract, Charles drew up his lists of considerations *pro* and *con,* and came out with a decision in favor of marrying. It would be pleasanter, good for the health, but a terrible loss of time, especially if one had to go walking with a wife daily. Still, to be alone would be worse. Finally he concluded: "There is many a happy slave."[31]

Their first child was born before the end of 1839, and nine more children were born during the next sixteen years. They lived a quiet, secluded life, giving up all the excitements which in Charles's younger days he had enjoyed. But his health did not improve. The notations of his unwellness and the stays in sanatoria and hydrotherapeutic establishments increased in frequency during Emma's childbearing period.

[64]

There was no quick relief from symptoms after the birth of the last child. But some reduction in the periods in sanatoria and a generally greater ease did gradually become apparent. He was a devoted father and frankly surprised at the elation that overtook him in regard to his children.[32] But he regarded the early years of his marriage as the least scientifically productive of his life. It took him three years to prepare for publication his work on coral reefs, which he began again and again. His confidence in his scientific ability was often in eclipse. In this respect he was behaving in a somewhat feminine fashion, for it is in women that biological creativeness seems chiefly to come into collision with intellectual and artistic creativity. Characteristically, however, he was observing his baby with a semidetached as well as with a loving eye, and studying its every movement, as publications many years later were to show.[33]

Of the ten children seven were to survive to adult life. For the second child, Anne Elizabeth, who died at the age of ten, he showed a frank and natural grief. The death of the third child, Mary Eleanor, at three weeks, is recorded but scantily, occurring as it did in a period of several deaths and illnesses in the family. Charles at the age of thirty-three suddenly looked old. Sixteen years later, the youngest child, named Charles for his father and Waring for his grandfather, was to die at the age of two,[34] just at the time when the father was most involved in the pressure to publish the *Origin of Species* because of the appearance of Wallace's work. It is an interesting coincidence in time that the publication of Darwin's greatest works and the flowering of his influence and fame began at this period when his procreative functions no longer bore fruit. When at forty-one Charles Darwin lost his father, he was too ill to attend the funeral, and years later he made one of those revealing slips of memory, misstating the date of the death, an error which he could never understand.

Emma Darwin was a good wife for Charles, a conservative, kind, and essentially motherly woman who filled a heroic role with great staunchness. She did not complain about his illnesses, and carried the family with fortitude and strength. She was his cousin, the youngest in a large family of Wedgwood cousins, the children of a favorite uncle. She was surely the representative of the lost mother whom he could not in the least remember. She was said to have been a pretty young woman, animated, cheerful, and poised. A picture of her at thirty-one would confirm this.[35] In the family she had always been paired with her sister Frances, a plain little girl, not overly bright and rather shy. The two children were the pets of the family, nicknamed the Doveleys. As they grew up they seemed to share a compulsion neurosis between them. Fanny became the overly methodical woman, who listed and sorted most of the things she worked with or knew, whereas Emma tended to be helter-skelter or at least unorganized. So Fanny was nick-named, *Mrs. Pedigree,* while Emma was called *Miss Slip-Shod.*

Emma never did become really tidied up, and

Charles, who had a bit of the Mr. Pedigree in him, early made up his mind that he would not be irked by his wife's disregard of order and details. Since Charles and Emma had ten children, each may in his own way have had a fairly heroic job. There were, however, great tenderness and mutual appreciation in the marriage, though possibly without intense excitement. For all her untidiness Emma was capable, wrote a neat hand, was a good needlewoman and horsewoman, as well as being adept at archery. She was fond of music, and played daily for her own pleasure, although she was not an accomplished musician. She had faith in and great respect for her husband's ability, and in general took excellent care of him.

In the matter of religion, she seems to have had a quietly difficult time. According to her daughter, Henrietta, she was not only sincerely religious but definite in her beliefs. On her insistence the children were brought up according to the Unitarian creed, although they were baptized and confirmed in the Church of England. Especially in her early married life it distressed her to realize that her husband did not share her faith, and she wanted to think that all Charles's suffering was "from God's hands, to prepare for a future State"![36] Her attitudes may have contributed to her husband's conflict and extreme caution in expressing antireligious beliefs. After his death, too, she was conscientiously concerned about what would give offense if published, and may have exercised a mild censorship.

She was never quite at ease with her father-in-law. "There [i.e., at his home] all was orderly and correct, and everyone must conform to the Doctor's views of what was right. He was extremely kind and [she] was attached to him, but she never felt quite at ease in his presence. No one must speak so that he did not hear. A boy was naturally uncongenial to the Doctor. He was cautious, even timid in bodily dangers though with great moral fearlessness. . . . No one could have been more devoted and more reverent than my father [Charles]. What his father did or thought was to him absolutely true, right and wise" (Henrietta's account).[37]

That life was hard as well as giving a qualified and deep happiness to Emma Darwin is told in her face. A picture of her, after fourteen years of marriage,[38] shows a careworn face with tightening of the lips and around the mouth, but calm, gentle eyes. This picture resembles more the one at seventy-three,[39] and even the one at eighty-eight[40] than it does the early one when she was beginning her marriage at thirty-one. It is probable that in the marriage Charles progressively repressed any strong show of disagreement, and gave way before the strength of her religious beliefs. This would have the effect, unconsciously, of aligning her with his father in certain respects in Charles Darwin's mind and feeling, even though she was of quite a different make-up. Darwin had such strong reaction formations against realizing any aggression that he was overly tender and gentlemanly in his conscious behavior, until his neurosis would incapacitate him and cause him to retire from active contact with others.[41]

Charles's younger sister, Catherine, who had been considered so promising a child, remained an uncomfortable spinster until her fifties, when she married Charles Langton, who had previously been married to her aunt Charlotte Wedgwood, who had died a year earlier. Catherine only lived two and a half years after her marriage. Fanny Wedgwood, the other half of Emma's pair, died after a short illness at the age of twenty-six, some seven years before Emma married Charles Darwin.

The Butlers, like the Darwins, came of yeoman stock. During the early nineteenth century some members had branched out into the arts and sciences. Heavily directive, disciplinary attitudes of fathers toward sons seemed to prevail in Butler's family, unrelieved by softening maternal influences. Samuel Butler's father and grandfather were clergyman rather than doctors. The Samuel Butler who as headmaster built up the Shrewsbury School from a nearly defunct state to become one of the leading schools of England was grandfather to Samuel Butler of the controversy. He was an energetic, fundamentally fair-minded man of great tenacity, who was capable of living thirty-eight years without speaking to his assistant headmaster. The latter had been appointed contrary to his wishes and held tenure for life. Dr. Butler communicated through official memoranda, reputedly without once losing his temper.[42]

His only son, Thomas, was neither as brilliant nor as energetic as his father, and may have suffered as the sons of clergymen and schoolmasters often do, in having to be constantly on display to parishioners and parents of other pupils.[43] Thomas wanted to enter the Navy, but was urged into the Church by his father, and achieved an adequate but not greatly distinguished career. Our Samuel Butler was the elder of his two sons, and there were two sisters as well. The parents and two daughters seemed to form a compact group —smug, righteous, and ready to apply their procrustean standards generally.

The grandfather died on the younger Samuel's fourth birthday, as a result of which his small gifts were taken away from him, or at least so he recalled. That he resented the loss of the grandfather is suggested by his inability to have any kind of feeling contact with the actual memory or with a fantasy image of this man, whose namesake he was. Only late in life, at an age when he might have become a grandfather himself, did he discover his grandfather and become consciously fascinated with him. In this and in other respects his story has some resemblances to that of Darwin, for he was not considered especially bright or promising. Yet his picture of himself was probably different, for he described Ernest Pontifex in *The Way of All Flesh*, admittedly a self-portrait, as able to read by the age of three, and write after a fashion; and learning Latin and doing rule-of-three sums by four. His attitude toward his parents was to become one of insistent bitterness, but with a profound longing for affection which paradoxically caused him to make the most provocative demands on them and then be outraged when they did not comply. Thus as an adult he meticulously sent them copies of his books which he knew would offend them, and was bitter when they did not read what he had written. Even at the age of forty-seven he wrote that his father had never liked him, and that he could recall no time without fear and dislike on his side, too.[44] The attachment was unending. If Butler believed himself tormented by his father, he could never give up tormenting himself with the thoughts of his disappointment. He started writing his autobiographical novel in 1873 (at thirty-seven), a little after the time of his two visits to Darwin. But it was not published for thirty years. He had withheld it lest it offend other members of his family. Butler's mother seemed to play a singularly meager role in his life, appearing rather as part of the "they," the parents who condemned him when he hungered for recognition and approval, but on his own terms. She was described by her second cousin, Mrs. Richard S. Garnett, as the "most devotedly obsequious wife in all England."

If Samuel Butler resented the restrictions of his parents' demands, he reproduced them in the rigid, almost ritualistic arrangements of his personal life. Already in his early thirties he was living in monastic simplicity, with a schedule for rising, eating, brushing his hair a hundred strokes each morning, smoking a given number of cigarettes each day, and carefully rationing his time for painting, writing, and his music.[45] Even his weekly visits to a prostitute were arranged with reliable regularity.[46] John Butler Yeats, who was a fellow art student at Heatherley's Art School, remembered him as a man who disapproved of marriage but liked women because he found them good-natured. He had admitted a little shyly to a weakness of the flesh, and confessed that he had "a little needlewoman" whom he visited and to whom he had given a sewing machine.[47]

In contrast to Darwin, Butler never became in the least a family man, and never married. There were, however, three women in his life, and three men besides Darwin. The latter was the only person to whom he turned (predominantly in his writing) for fifteen to twenty years with a reverential admiration, and in whom he seemed to seek a kind, sympathetic god-father until, disappointed and angry, he turned back to God. His more tender and sustained relationships were with men, and were marked by a stubbornly enduring paternalism which he so craved for himself.

In New Zealand he found, not the ideal wife whom at that time he still thought he might discover,[48] but another kind of ideal in the person of Charles Paine Pauli, a little younger than himself, and, according to Butler, "a fine handsome fellow . . . everything I should like myself to be but know very well that I am not."[49] Butler practically adopted Pauli, who was sick and without funds, and brought him back to England. Butler came to recognize that he used Pauli to substitute for his very poor image of himself, but

he was not as definite about other aspects of the relationship. Pauli continued to be supported, at first
largely and then only partly by Butler. He lived by
himself and after a time refused to see Butler except
at regularly appointed luncheons when he collected
his remittance and indicated his need. Butler must
not even have his address. This incredible relationship continued for thirty-two years when, with Pauli's
death in 1897, Butler was to discover that Pauli was
earning a respectable income on his own, enhanced
by contributions from others whom he had charmed
as much as he had Butler.

The relationship can be understood as the complementary interaction of Pauli's psychopathy with
the severest disturbances in Butler's character. Butler
was a small man, physically gauche, who wore his
clothes badly and gained no self-assurance through
his considerable intellectual attractions. Pauli was
superficial, but in New Zealand at least was generally well liked and looked up to. He was neither
original nor really intellectual, but cut a good figure.
These things might also be said of Butler's father.
Butler behaved toward Pauli as he would have liked
all-understanding and enduring parents to behave
toward him. He wrote: "I had felt from the beginning that my intimacy with Pauli was only superficial. I perceived . . . that I bored him. . . . He
cared little for literature and nothing for philosophy,
music and the arts. . . . He liked society and I hated
it. Moreover he was at times very irritable and would
find continual fault with me. . . . Devoted to him as

[73]

I continued to be for many years, these years were very unhappy as well as happy ones."[50] And in a further memorandum written after Pauli's death, Butler referred to the whole affair as a squalid, miserable story. He was convinced that if he had withdrawn from Pauli, the latter would have blown out his brains; but that if Pauli had sorrowed and then had died from one of his frequent attacks of bronchitis, he would himself have been haunted by the fear of responsibility for Pauli's death.[51] Nothing could speak more clearly of the pitch of Butler's ambivalence to his father. In this same memorandum Butler compared his enduring of Pauli for thirty-two years with his grandfather's enduring of the assistant headmaster to whom he did not speak for thirty-eight years. Nor did he miss noting that Pauli died exactly on the eleventh anniversary of his own father's death, on December 29. Strangely enough, Pauli's father had died on the day after the Canon's death.

Butler's relationship to his two younger brothers may also have contributed to the complexity and perseverance of his support of Pauli. Samuel Butler's early memories, like Darwin's, were of death. Eight months before his grandfather's death when he was four, he had experienced the death of a younger brother at six months.[52] He always remembered this as though the naked body of the dead infant had been exposed to him, and was wont to refer to the child as the only member of the family with whom he had not quarreled.[53] The brother, Tom, whose life is generally such a silent area in the official Butler annals, was somewhere between Samuel and the dead brother in age, and was probably about as much younger than Samuel as Pauli was. At least he and Samuel were at school and college together, as excerpts from Sam's letters show.

Philip Henderson, a more recent (1953) biographer of Butler, has brought out facts in regard to Tom which do not appear in the *Memoirs*. As late as 1879, when Butler's grievance against Darwin was mounting, he was importuning his father for financial aid, and felt that he had been outwitted in the matter of some property. The controversy with his father was even more complex than that with Darwin. The vigilant father had learned enough of Pauli to discover that Pauli had an income of his own, and to resent being asked to contribute to him through Sam. Sam, disbelieving this, halfway convinced his father too. At any rate, it is one of the few times when in this troubled father-son relationship sympathy can go readily to Canon Butler. Just at this time, the errant Tom turned up with a Belgian woman, apparently intent on blackmailing his father. The latter was so distraught at his second son's life that he even thought of trying to have a guardian appointed. Tom, who was then separated from his wife and family, threatened to disappear altogether, which he did four years later, and six years before his death in 1885. Tom Butler was said to have hated his father "with a fury which it would be hard to surpass," and in return the Canon said: "I don't care about knowing where he is, so long as we hear of his death."

Samuel Butler had never liked his brother Tom. But it is still possible that in Pauli he reclaimed an acceptable version of him. A picture of Tom, taken in 1865, shows an unattractively gross and portly man.[54] The desperate years, 1879–1881, when the controversies were going on and Canon Butler was struggling with both his sons, was a time when Samuel felt impelled to rewrite *The Way of All Flesh*.

But by this time (1878) Butler had already met Henry Festing Jones, who was destined to be the second man in his life on whom he lavished tender, faithful affection. While it was a slowly developing friendship, Butler came to idealize him extravagantly, and later referred to him as the ablest man he had ever known, thus putting him above Darwin. Festing Jones appears to have been interested in painting and in music, but without special talent. His greatest contribution was his admirably carefully written *Memoirs of Samuel Butler* after the latter's death. He had become Butler's background and almost his Boswell. In return he was supported by Butler, who had now inherited money from his father.

The deaths of Darwin (1882), Tom Butler (1885), Canon Butler (1886), and Samuel's friend Miss Savage (1885) all occurred then within a period of four years. He had become more or less alienated from them all before their deaths, and his loneliness increased his dependence on Jones, while the inheritance eased the practical pressures of his life. Butler gave Jones an allowance, so that he need no longer work except as a companion and assistant to himself.

[76]

Jones, who had studied law, even as Pauli had done earlier, had worked as a lawyer's clerk but did not like it, and had suffered under the demands of his widowed mother on whom he had been reluctantly partially dependent. Butler also paid up what he "owed" Pauli. He bought himself a new hand basin and new hairbrushes. Otherwise he did not immediately change his way of life. But one change occurred spontaneously; for years he had suffered from attacks of giddiness with severe noises in the ear which often interfered with his work. Whatever the nature of these symptoms, they cleared up soon after his father's death.[55]

It may be surmised that Samuel Butler's oedipal jealousy was expressed largely in feelings of physical inferiority toward his father, who was a bigger man and more handsome, according to conventional standards. He was surely brighter than his father, and knew it, but never freed this realization from his demands that his father should recognize it also. The whole relationship had become pathetically degraded into wrangles about money. He never made any money on his books, either, which were generally published at his own expense. Although he always hoped for a profit he would queer himself with both publisher and public. When Canon Butler died, Samuel was at his bedside, and held the dying man's head. He was relieved that death occurred without a struggle, but he quickly remarked that it takes money to die in comfort. Butler's acrimoniousness toward life showed in his face; there was a slightly Mephis-

tophelian or goatish slant to his expression suggestive
of Shaw, but without the airy lightness of the latter.[56]

Within a few months after his father's death, Butler hired and practically adopted his third man, Alfred Emery Cathie, aged twenty-two, the son of a
Cockney charwoman. Alfred became half son and
half nurse, with secretarial duties thrown in to boot.
Butler also played the Pygmalion role, taking Alfred
with him on cultural tours to the Continent, attempt-
ing to teach him about music and astronomy, and to
educate him generally, an enterprise for which Alfred was less than wholeheartedly enthusiastic. On
the other hand, acting as nursery governess, Alfred
told Butler when to change his underwear, when to
buy a new hat, when to quit composing and go for a
walk, and even instructed Jones when to take Butler
to the theater. Alfred bullied him somewhat, and left
admonitory notes, affectionately threatening disap-
proval in case of disobedience. In return, Butler repeated Alfred's saucy remarks much like a parent
boasting of a precocious child, and declared himself
prouder of Alfred's letters than of all his own books
put together. When Alfred married seven years later,
Butler bore it reasonably well, even accepting with
equanimity grandparenthood, which arrived five
months after the wedding. Alfred stayed with him until his death, and Butler's last words were to ask if
Alfred had brought the checkbook.

Perhaps Butler's acceptance of Alfred's marriage
was a bit easier, not only because Canon Butler's
death had opened the way for his son to succeed him

[78]

in a more outspokenly paternal attitude, but, in addition, Butler and Jones had already found a son for
themselves. The demand for a son had become ur-
gently conscious, and was gratified for a time by an
intense friendship with a young Swiss, Hans Faesch.
The two older men hovered over the ailing Hans
with every solicitude, and took him on regular and
almost ritualistically repetitious Sunday walks in the
country for nearly two years. In his notebooks Butler
was frank to admit that he would like a son, but
never a wife. Fortunately, when Alfred's progeny was
born, and the child was a boy, Butler could feel himself a proper grandfather. He was mellower anyway,
and had only recently discovered his grandfather, the
elder Samuel Butler, against whom he had earlier
had some prejudice even when he had been impelled
to reach out and annex Darwin's grandfather.

When Hans Faesch went to the Orient and settled
in Indo-China, Butler, grieving deeply, wrote a poem
"In Memoriam," which seemed to embarrass the
young man somewhat. Butler explained in a letter
that he wanted to make a permanent record of the
friendship of the three men, to set them together in
a kind of ring where they might stay in the hearts of
those who knew them.[57] He frequently addressed
Faesch as his dear son, and he instructed Alfred simply to say the magic word *Hans* to him if he were
irritable, and the sun would shine again.

In another letter, he expresses the same familiar
rescue offer as with Pauli and Jones: "[If] when you
get to Singapore you find you have made a serious

mistake . . . especially suppose the doctors . . . tell [you] that you will do yourself mischief to stay . . . and [you] do not wish to apply to your mother for fear of burdening her, then, my dear Hans, let me beseech you in the name of all the affection a dear father can bear to a very dear son . . . apply to me . . . without delay in whatever way will ensure your getting the answer quickest, which you will immediately receive. I mean *draw on me at once for your passage money and necessary expenses and come home.*"[58] Hans Faesch apparently, like Jones, was the ailing son of a widow.

Butler not only wanted to be a father to this boy, but there is more than a hint that he increasingly wanted to take over the role of a mother. His jokes of this period betray a frankly feminine aspect to his feelings. For example, on the Sunday walks to Gadshill where the three men stopped regularly to drink beer and pick up fresh eggs at an inn run by three women, Butler liked to joke that he felt like a woman in the family way when he left with his basket of eggs, fearful of breaking them by bumping into some obstacle.[59] It was at this time, too, that he became engaged in another controversy, this time to prove that not Homer but a woman was the author of the *Odyssey*.

Even before the Hans Faesch period, he had begun translating into English prose first the *Odyssey* (published in 1900) and then the *Iliad* (published in 1898), at first with an idea of collaborating with Jones on an opera. This led into unexpected channels. It took him back to his grandfather, the great classics scholar, and led him further to the idea of the feminine authorship of the *Odyssey*—a point of view which he defended zealously. In 1896, he published a two-volume biography of his grandfather, *Life and Letters of Dr. Samuel Butler,* and in 1897 came *The Authoress of the Odyssey.* His thesis was based on a careful study of the style of the poem: its expressions, similes, and figures of speech in general, as well as its descriptions, the range of interest and knowledge of the author.[60] Again he had difficulty getting a publisher, probably because in his talk, at least, he played up the controversial nature of his presentation, and because he was not taken very seriously by the public anyway.

But we have delayed any discussion of Butler's relationship to women, and especially to the three who were at all important to him. One was an intellectual woman, one was a beauty, and the third was a reliable French prostitute. He probably met the first, Eliza Mary Anne Savage, in 1867, while he was still a student at Heatherley's Art School. She was intelligent, witty, and sometimes tiresome, not attractive physically, and also lame. The friendship did not develop at once, but it continued with fluctuations until the time of her death in 1885. He accompanied his conviction that she wanted to marry him by a caution amounting at times to rudeness. She acted as a kind of literary monitor to him: he sent her practically everything he wrote and, although rather prejudiced in his favor, she often offered good suggestions and criticisms. Even her enthusiasms for his writing would send him scurrying into retreat; and he seemed quite unaware of her probable sensitivities. In the end, during a period when he had been somewhat out of touch with her, she entered a hospital for an operation for cancer. Unaware of her illness, he wrote her a long letter humorously lamenting the deaths of so many of his friends just when they had become really useful to him. She died a few days later without ever seeing him again. Then he wrote his sister that "he had never known any woman to approach her in brilliancy and goodness."[61] It was she who had prodded and encouraged him into writing *The Way of All Flesh*.

Isabella Zanetti was the daughter of the hotel-keeper at Arona Maggiore. When he saw her first she was quite young and very beautiful. Butler felt deeply moved and thought in terms of how impossible it would be to marry her. He left very soon and did not return for seven years. In the meantime his way of life with Festing Jones had been established, and he wished to show her to this friend, who declared himself also in love with her at first sight.[62] But the two Englishmen left quite comfortably the next day. At fifty-nine, he saw her again when she kept a hotel in Florence. He was sentimentally faithful to her memory now that he was no longer endangered by her in person. Not much of her life, nor any of her thoughts, are revealed in the biographies.

"Madame," the name by which Butler habitually called Lucie Dumas, came into his life only a few months after his meeting with Isabella. She was only twenty-one, a French girl who had set herself up in London. Butler picked her up on the street. She already had a son who was being supported in France by his father on condition that she remain outside of France. Jones, who knew her well, tells little about her except that she was absolutely trustworthy and had a heart of gold. It was only after he had known her for fifteen years that Butler allowed her to have his name and address. Then in some ritualistic recognition of their long time together, he brought her to his rooms to tea sometimes. His behavior here is strangely like that of Pauli,[63] who refused to give him his address but would lunch with him regularly. "Madame" was the needlewoman to whom Butler had early given a sewing machine in his confession to Yeats. It was Alfred Cathie who in his old age revealed what a truly regularized relationship existed between Madame, Butler, and Jones. According to him, Butler visited her each Wednesday, and Jones went on Tuesdays. Each gave her a pound a week, including holidays. The alliance lasted for twenty years, and was terminated by her death from tuberculosis in her early forties (1892).[64] Jones also makes it clear that during these years she had no rivals with Butler, though she had other clients. She is credited with having said of Butler: "He knows everything; he knows nothing; he is a poet."

Butler's interests flowed in many directions. He was writer, painter, composer, and undertook to be a natural philosopher and classics scholar as well. His novel, perhaps the only one he had in him, *The Way of All Flesh,* won not only recognition but fame for him. But this arrived posthumously. *Erewhon,* on the other hand, was read rather widely immediately after it was published. It appeared anonymously. As his cousin unflatteringly predicted, as soon as the true authorship was known the sales dropped almost to the base line. He did have a short period of lionization, however.

Butler's talent for painting was not great. In fact, according to John Butler Yeats, a fellow art student, it was distressingly lacking. He wished to paint after the fashion of Bellini, but was pathetically cramped. He was, however, socially distinctly the upper-class English gentleman among the art students, correcting their pronunciation and tidying up their manners. One of his paintings, however, found a place in the Tate Gallery, also posthumously. One might think that he was a man divided by a multiplicity of interests, and the problem of making a focused choice. This was not the major difficulty.

In music, as well as in other fields of creative endeavor, a certain constricting combination of attitudes closing in on the freedom of his creativity was apparent. First he patterned himself on a model against whom he ultimately turned. He rarely was impelled to create except to prove that some authority was wrong. He was in this sense a militant savior, dedicated to undoing special wrongs which he felt had been committed. He might worship until he saw the clay feet, but then he must set people straight.

In music he had one god, Handel, whom he worshiped devoutly. He seemed fearful of having his feelings exploited by writers of emotional music. Toward them he was disparaging and ridiculing. If Handel had been alive, Butler might have turned on him as he did on Darwin.

As it was, he and Jones (1884–1888) collaborated on a cantata dealing with one subject that Handel never touched, viz., fluctuations on the Stock Exchange, a condition about which Butler had firsthand knowledge. The cantata followed two years of writing gavottes, fugues, minuets, etc., as much in the manner of Handel as possible. In it, the proverbial shepherd boy, Narcissus, strays to London, loses his money, but in the end is rescued by a good godmother who dies and leaves him a substantial legacy. Thereupon he bursts into song:

> I never knew her worth till now
> A hundred thousand pound!
> Small is my loss indeed, I vow,
> Compared with what I've found.
>
> Oh! had she known I'd lost so much
> Or ere her pulse was still,
> Her testament had not been such
> She would have changed her will.[65]

It is an almost autobiographical expression of his hopes and fantasies.

The writing of this trivial cantata had led the two friends to consider collaboration in doing an opus in the Handelian manner, based on Ulysses. It was the rereading of the *Odyssey* and the *Iliad* in preparation for this that led him to his work on the authorship of the *Odyssey*, to rediscover his grandfather, and then to engage in writing the biography of the elder Samuel Butler. As these two projects occupied the next few years, the oratorio *Ulysses* was not really completed at the time of his death in 1902, and was not published until 1904.

Application of the Thesis
to the Clinical Material

How, THEN, MIGHT the forces at work in producing the controversy between Samuel Butler and Charles Darwin be understood—in terms of their individual life settings, personal experiences and relationships, and the pressures of their special period; and not merely on the merits of their arguments? We would put the emphasis in this presentation on the reciprocal impact of the intrapsychic struggles of the two men, since it is important in itself as well as furnishing an especially good illustration of our thesis. It must be stressed that while the creative individual responds in special ways to the ordinary patterns of personal relationships with heightened force and vividness, he is also an unusually sensitive receptor, reflector, and sometimes a condenser of the currents of his time.

Although a generation apart in age, Darwin and Butler came from the same general social background and locality, with similar life experiences, and specific, though not close, relationships between their families. The combined span of their lives (1809–

1902) approximates closely the life period of Queen Victoria; their lives were encompassed by and expressive of that remarkable era. A study of the life of the Queen gives one a feeling of having seen a magnified and emblazoned version of the households of the Darwins and the Butlers, in all their solid virtues, their complacencies, their piety, their rebellious sons, and their relative unawareness of aesthetic values. It seems a significant though frequently overlooked fact that during the very long reign of the carefully self-centered Queen seven threats were made against her life, all but two by adolescent youths carrying unloaded pistols.

In the eighteenth century, the pursuit of botany had become a weekday hobby of the English clergy. Collecting and identifying a great variety of plants joined them to their more daring contemporaries, who had only recently been discovering and naming whole areas of the globe, and now in the nineteenth century were bringing back samples of plants, animals, and minerals, both for study by scientific and amateur naturalists and for the adornment of curio collections. The period of discovery and exploration was succeeded by a period of naming and classification, which fit in well with the general orderliness of the Victorian era and the security of family life.

Darwin and Butler arose from and rebelled against this comfortable but oppressive background, probably because they were men of talent whose restless, inquiring minds refused to accept the personal and stultifying dictates of their immediate fathers. Darwin was a man of genius—inherently more gifted than Butler, whose talent is difficult to assess. It would also appear that Darwin's family background offered him a more intellectually stimulating array of paternal models with whom to identify and fortify himself. Both men had illustrious grandfathers of whom fantasy images may have influenced them powerfully, though unconsciously. Both had fathers who, having suffered tyranny at the hands of these same grandfathers, turned the tables and in more cramped and less distinguished ways attempted to force their sons as their fathers had forced them. Rebellion against Victorian standards was gradually gaining strength along with the vast social and economic changes of the industrial revolution. It was the peculiar fate and gift of these two men, each in his own way, to implement and promote the revolt against God-given authoritarianism and stratified structure which characterized alike Victorian society and the Victorian family.

Darwin's personal revolt was first apparent in his defection from medicine, the profession of his father and his grandfather, and then from theology, which was his father's second choice for him. His turning to the natural sciences and finally, especially, to biology, seemed to have its roots in boyhood collecting hobbies. But it was rooted even more deeply in powerful drives to understand the mysteries and magic in sex and death, and in the need not to be swept away by his own sadomasochistic fantasies and impulses. With increasing patience and meticulously careful observations, he amassed an enormous number of facts from which convictions of evolution as contrary to divine creation of species gradually emerged. "Disbelief [in God]," he said later, "crept over me at a very slow rate, but at last was complete. The rate was so slow that I felt no distress" (see Appendix, note 7). Nor did he seem really aware of his hostility to his personal father, which was betrayed, however, by the unfailingly exaggerated and superlative terms in which he spoke of Dr. Robert Darwin, except for a few timid complaints of the possible injustice of his father's derogation of him. In this respect his behavior was in contrast to that of his sisters, who among themselves and with their cousins could both suffer and mock the elder Darwin's tyranny. The massive aggression which had to be repressed contributed to his obsessional neurosis and the associated imposing array of somatic symptoms which so innocently incapacitated him, dominating his life and that of his whole household.

While his unusual capacity for neurotic denial made some margin of life possible, still unconscious hostility almost surely penetrated into the affective background of his work, which was always upsetting to him. Two or three hours of work a day might prove so disturbingly exciting as to produce overwhelming fatigue, and even talking for an hour could produce insomnia. Thus the creative endeavors which gave him such passionate satisfaction paradoxically sent him to hydrotherapeutic sanatoria for days and weeks at a time. He was able to keep the *content* of his work almost wholly free from neurotic inroads, although he was generally unable simply and directly to admit that his theories were such as to overthrow the Victorian belief in Divine Creation.

Some degree of feminine identification probably arose from his early obligatory submissiveness to his father, his extremely close association with his younger sister, and his mourning for his mother, with a consequent prolonged identification with her. This would naturally lead to a bisexual conflict during the years on the *Beagle* where he was entirely with men and shared quarters with the righteously sadistic Captain. This conflict expressed itself subsequently, especially after his marriage, in his increasing timidity in gatherings of men. Scientific meetings became almost intolerably exciting to him.

Various psychiatric clinical studies of Charles Darwin's illness have been made. With one exception (Alvarez, 1943), these interpreters (Good, 1954a, 1954b; Hermann, 1927; Hubble, 1943, 1946, 1954; Kempf, 1920) have agreed that the core of Darwin's neurosis lay in his extreme but unconscious hostility to his father. The psychoanalytic treatise of Hermann stresses Darwin's preoccupation with time as a special theme in the rebellion against his father. Darwin's sisters seem to have had the same feeling in nicknaming their father "The Tide." Indeed, Father Time with his scythe is the agent of birth and death, even as the Doctor was. Darwin's neurosis also defied his father's therapeutic wisdom, which he praised so highly. The slight relief he could get was from irregular practitioners for whom Dr. Robert Darwin had limited sympathy.

Although the family pattern and some of the elements of Butler's neurosis were similar to Darwin's, yet his character was quite different. His hostility to his father was direct, outspoken, and almost incessant. He lumped his parents together; but the shafts of his aggressive attacks were aimed almost entirely at his father. Fewer details of his early life are known than was the case with Darwin, perhaps because his strife was patent and alienated so many that relatives did not leave naïvely approving accounts of his childhood. There are indications that he may have felt physically inferior to his father. In adult life his manner was that of a man with little confidence in his physical impressiveness. He too renounced the profession of his father and grandfather and demanded his father's financial help in the pursuit of the arts. Canon Butler, like Dr. Robert Darwin, had little faith in his talented son, and said so with equal asperity.

Butler never married. He lived a cramped, somewhat embittered and methodical life, dominated by his relation to his father, which he repeatedly reversed and lived out in relation to younger men. All of them were taller than he and in their own ways more personable, though much less competent. His bitterness and compulsive need to attack authority invaded the very content of his creativeness, no matter what medium he used. He had some intimation of how much he was bound by his need for invective and by his narcissism, for he spoke often of feeling that he was unimaginative in that he could see others only in the narrow personal terms of himself.

Yet the work which brought him great posthumous fame, the novel *The Way of All Flesh,* was highly personal, a superb arraignment of the Victorian family—his family—in full-dress hypocrisy. It was not published until after his death, since paradoxically he did not wish to subject this same family to the force of his attack. It won its way partly because it was brooded over with such intensity that, although highly personal, it burst the bounds of the merely personal, and partly because by the time of its publication, the Victorian era had passed and the twentieth century had begun. It is doubtful whether it would have caught on earlier. The times were not ready for it. Besides, Butler's talent for antagonizing people was such that nothing he wrote was really very successful while he lived. If he published anonymously, sales dropped as soon as the true authorship became known.

But when Butler was still in his twenties and in the first passion of revolt, he had encountered Darwin's ideas and had fallen in love with their author. It was an awe-inspired attachment, and lasted for more than a decade before its nether side of hostility became obvious and demanding. The infantile love which Butler craved so much and tried unsuccessfully and with anguished disillusionment to get from his father and the Church's God, he was at first ready to bestow on Darwin, whose theories seemed to be

[93]

toppling the stronghold of Canon Butler and others like him. If his creative strivings had been less bound to his personal demand for an all-embracing understanding, he might have been able to use Darwin as a father ideal who would serve as a patron. But he could not relinquish his claim for the kind of care which only an omnipotent father-god, combining mother and father, could give. He did not want to give up his conception of God at all, only to find Him again in full intellectual regalia. Nor was Butler misled by Darwin's obsessional hesitancy about declaring independence of God. He seemed to know that Darwin was firm and could not give him what he was seeking.

This came upon him very slowly, when he found to his chagrin that what he had written was anti-Darwin even while he had thought that he was supporting evolution and the origin of the species through natural selection. The latter was most devastating, for it meant to him a world built too much by chance rather than under the protection of an omniscient guiding intellect which might reward with special and inheritable growth the individual's wish and effort toward adaptation. He conceived of all plants, animals, and even inorganic substances as having such wills in the direction of adaptation. In his reading and brooding he came upon Lamarck, Buffon, Linnaeus, and Erasmus Darwin, and he liked them better than Charles Darwin with his destructive emphasis on change.

Presently he found himself angry and feeling

cheated by Darwinism, even as he had originally been by the Church and his parents. His anger found a justification in facts—events which were true but were hardly a basis for the accusations of scientific duplicity which he brought against the bewildered Darwin. The one-sided controversy continued, for Darwin refrained from answering and neither one really understood quite clearly what the other was talking about. After Darwin's death, the public controversy subsided, but the rancor and sense of grievance persisted throughout Butler's life, as his notes and letters show.

The controversy was the medium through which Butler attempted to rid himself of Darwin if he could not accept or subjugate him. To a degree, he attempted to replace Charles Darwin with his grandfather Erasmus, whose cause he dramatically espoused. This was Butler's last attempt to find a patron. Already years before he had found another method of dealing with the problem—through becoming the patron himself and adopting protégés. But none of the protégés was remarkable. Though he praised them extravagantly, none of them could realize for him. His underlying attachment to his father and his father's God was apparent when, after his father's death, the noises in one ear which had bothered him for years soon disappeared.

Appendix

The Thesis

1. The title *Fathers and Sons* suggested itself for this study, since this is the pivotal relationship focused on. But the fact that *Fathers and Sons,* or in its singular form *Father and Son,* is a title which has been often used seemed somewhat to detract from the specificity of its significance and paradoxically to emphasize its general importance to writers. Turgenev wrote of *Fathers and Sons,* Edmund Gosse called his autobiography *Father and Son,* while Dostoyevsky considered it as a possible title for *The Brothers Karamazov.* It is the heading for the first chapter in at least several autobiographies.

2. The basic inborn characteristics of the creative person were enumerated by me in a paper on "The Childhood of the Artist" (1957). In the few years since then, my continued reading and study of biographies have brought me support in these formulations in so far as the latter have helped to clarify and make sense of many apparent contradictions and previously murky and puzzling matters. Most of my reading has been devoted to study of the lives of writers, but it has not been entirely so limited.

3. The phrase "regression in the service of the ego" has been found so useful that it is incorporated into psychoanalytic literature rather generally. In chapter I, Approaches to Art, in *Psychoanalytic Explorations of Art,* E. Kris states: "Inspiration—the 'divine release from ordinary ways of man,' a state of 'creative madness' (Plato), in which the ego controls the primary process and puts it into its service—needs to be contrasted with the opposite, the psychotic condition, in which the ego is overwhelmed by the primary process. The difference is clearest where the relation to the public is concerned" (p. 60). Kris discusses the application of this conception of regression in ego service again in Chapter 5 on "The 'Creative Spell' in a Schizophrenic Artist" (p. 167) ; in Chapter 7 on "The Principles of Caricature" (pp. 197-198); and again in Chapter 10 on "Aesthetic Ambiguity" (p. 253), certainly an integral part of his theories of the psychodynamics of artistic creation. It may be seen that while I owe much of the stimulation of my interest in creativity to the influence of Kris, yet my own conception of the artist's relation to the collective alternates and to his creative products (these latter, at best, as true love gifts) varies somewhat from Kris's point of view regarding the essentially narcissistic character of the relation of the artist to his work (Kris, pp. 60-63). Certainly the two points of view are not wholly opposed. The difference is largely: (1) in the estimate of the ratio of narcissism to object relationship, a ratio which must vary greatly from individual to individual; and (2) in the degree of shift of psychic energy involved in the utilization of primary process in creative work. I had the benefit of discussing my own paper on "The Childhood of the Artist" with Kris immediately after writing it, and had

[97]

looked forward to further discussions, when his death made these impossible.

The Controversy

4. Basil Willey, Fellow of Pembroke College and King Edward VII Professor of English Literature in the University of Cambridge, has presented his view of Darwin's work, not merely for its influence on the biological sciences, but especially from the angle of its effect on the thought and feelings of the nineteenth century.

5. Clara Gruening Stillman is an American writer about whom little personal information is available. The biography of Samuel Butler seems to be her main published work. Appearing at a time when Butler's posthumous fame as the author of *The Way of All Flesh* was still at its height, it is an unusually thorough piece of work, written with a generally emotionally objective attitude about a man whose very character often elicited strong opposition or vehement defense.

6. Although Shaw lauded Butler heartily as "in his own department, the greatest writer of the latter half of the XIXth century," he had scant appreciation for some of Butler's later writing, and considered *Alps and Sanctuaries* "surely the silliest book ever written by a clever man."

7. Darwin's conflict concerning religion was handled by him through his separating it from his scientific views and considering that it was a completely private affair, so that he was reluctant to make any statement for publication. In 1879 he wrote Mr. J. Fordyce a letter which was published in 1883, i.e., after Darwin's death. "What my own views may be is a question of no consequence to

anyone but myself. But as you ask, I may state that my judgment often fluctuates. . . . In my most extreme fluctuations, I have never been an atheist in the sense of denying the existence of God. I think that generally (and more and more as I grow older), but not always, an agnostic would be the more correct description of my state of mind." In a letter of 1871 to Dr. F. E. Abbot of Cambridge, Massachusetts, he explained that the bad state of his health prevented him from feeling "equal to deep reflection on the deepest subject which can fill a man's mind." Repeatedly his answers to questions about religion start with statements that his ill-health has precluded his giving the matter as serious and profound consideration as it merits. One gains the impression that there is an inner connection between his ill-health and his difficulty in thinking of questions of religion.

In writing his *Autobiography* (1876), however, he recollects that during his first two years on the *Beagle* he gave much thought to religion, was quite orthodox, and suffered some teasing for quoting the Bible as an unanswerable authority on some point of morality. He then adds: "But I had gradually come by this time [i.e., 1836–1839] to see that the Old Testament was no more to be trusted than the sacred books of the Hindoos. The question then continually rose before my mind and would not be banished—is it credible that if God were now to make a revelation to the Hindoos, he would permit it to be connected with the belief in Vishnu, Siva, etc. as Christianity is connected with the Old Testament? This appeared to me utterly incredible. . . . But I was unwilling to give up my belief; . . . I can well remember often and often inventing day dreams of old letters between distinguished Romans, and manuscripts being discovered at

[99]

Pompeii or elsewhere, which confirmed in the most striking manner all that was written in the Gospels. But I found it more and more difficult with free scope given to my imagination to invent evidence which would suffice to convince me. Thus disbelief crept over me at a very slow rate but was at last complete. The rate was so slow that I felt no distress. . . ." He then recounts that in the days of the *Beagle* he had feelings—at least related to a deep inward conviction of God's presence when he stood awe-struck in a Brazilian forest—but that as years passed he lost this capacity for responsiveness. While he seemed to deplore this loss, he could actually no longer believe that inward conviction was proof of God's existence, and felt the admiration for Nature was really a sense of sublimity, whatever that was. (Quotations here are from F. Darwin's *Life and Letters of Charles Darwin,* 1911; Chapter on Religion, pp. 274-286.)

8. Erasmus A. Darwin, who was four to five years older than Charles, studied medicine at Edinburgh and took the degree of Bachelor of Medicine at Cambridge. He never practiced medicine, and settled down to a quiet unmarried life in London without any definite occupation. He was an intimate of the Carlyles and of Harriet Martineau. The two brothers were friendly but both handicapped by ill-health, which gradually increased the distance between London and Down House. The Charles Darwin family considered Erasmus as having a wit and playfulness similar to Charles Lamb's. Carlyle preferred his intellect to that of Charles, and felt there was "something of original and sarcastically ingenious in him—one of the sincerest, naturally truest and most modest of men." Charles felt that Carlyle did

not sufficiently appreciate his brother's most lovable nature. Erasmus admired the *Origin of Species* and considered it the most interesting book he had ever read. Each brother privately thought the other somewhat sad. Charles frequently called Erasmus "Poor old Ras"—and at the time of his death wrote: "He was not, I think, a happy man, and for many years did not value life, though never complaining," while Ras, on the other hand, after visits to the Charles Darwins, expressed to Mrs. Carlyle his relief at returning to London from "Down-at-the-Mouth." Erasmus died at seventy-seven, a year before Charles's death. (Notes here are from F. Darwin's *Life and Letters of Charles Darwin,* 1:20-22; 2:28, 404; and from Carlyle's *Reminiscences,* p. 433.)

9. The first part of this period (i.e., until his marriage in 1839) was one of unusual activity. Although he complained of occasional unwellness, he was not only doing his scientific work but serving as one of the Secretaries of the Geological Society, a duty which he would later have considered quite onerous, and he seemed to do considerable reading. It was in 1838 that he read Malthus's treatise on *Principles of Population* which helped to crystallize so much for him.

10. Professor Lyell—later Sir Charles Lyell—was professor of geology at Cambridge, and early became interested in Darwin when he entered Cambridge. He was a man of wide interests, having early developed an interest in natural history; later in geology. He then studied law but gave it up after two years to return to geology. His chief works were *The Principles of Geology* (3 Volumes, 1830–1833), which became a standard work, and *The Antiquity of Man* (1863).

[101]

11. Professor Hooker—later Sir Joseph Hooker—nine years younger than Darwin, was his friend throughout his mature life. He was a distinguished botanist and traveler. Together with Lyell he persuaded Darwin finally to publish his view on the origin of species.

12. Alfred Russel Wallace, co-discoverer with Darwin of the principles of evolution of species through natural selection, was nine years younger than "the master." He came from a family much less well established socially than either the Darwins or the Butlers, and somewhat impoverished by his father's impracticality. Next to the youngest of nine children, he lived in a simple village atmosphere until five, in Usk, Monmouthshire, near the Welsh border, and from then until fourteen at Hertford.

He did not seem to become intellectually awakened until, driven by economic pressures, he left home at fourteen to find an occupation. First he stayed for a few months in London with an older brother who was apprenticed to a master builder. He spent much time with the workmen employed there, and gained certain impressions of social and economic conditions in the metropolis which stayed with him throughout his lifetime. Then, as planned, he worked until he came of age under his oldest brother who was a surveyor. This work took him into many areas in Wales and southwestern England. At twenty his father died. At twenty-one, finding little surveying work to be done, he attempted, not too happily, to teach school. This enterprise was not much to his liking, and was soon interrupted by the death of his brother (the surveyor) and the need to help settle the latter's affairs. He had already come under the influence of Robert Owen, through whom his interests in socialism and in education were deepened. During the years as a surveyor, he was aroused to learn about geology, which in turn led to a really passionate concern with other aspects of natural history. During the period of teaching he had already paid attention to phrenology, a budding science of the time, and to mesmerism (hypnotism), and became convinced of his own special mesmeric powers.

About this same time he read Malthus's essay on *Principles of Population,* and also became acquainted with the young naturalist H. W. Bates, with whom he went on a trip of exploration to Brazil (1848–1852). On this trip Wallace suffered two severe blows: his younger brother, who had come out to join him, but was not really suited for the work, died of yellow fever in Para while waiting for the ship to return to England; and on his own return voyage, the ship was destroyed by fire. He and others were saved after spending a number of days in lifeboats. However, he lost almost his entire collection of biological specimens.

His articles and two books based on his trip brought him some support, so that in January, 1854 he set out on a voyage to Singapore and the Malay archipelago. By this time he was well aware of, and vastly interested in, Darwin's work. In 1855 he published an article on the "Law Which Regulated the Introduction of New Species," which Darwin recognized with warm praise. In 1858 he was pondering over the great problem of the origin of species (which had actually been with him in one form or another since 1847) when, during a sharp attack of malaria, the recollection of Malthus's essay came to him, after which it *flashed* upon him that the development of different species could come about through the principles of natural selection. During the next two nights he worked feverishly on writing an account of his views, which he then sent off to Darwin. It was this *flash* which had sufficient impact on Darwin to cause him to publish the *Origin of Species*. In 1870 came Wallace's contribution to the *Theory of Natural Selection,* in which he indicated that he differed from Darwin in that he thought man (with his capacity for intellect and morality) was unlike other animals in that his emergence was not due wholly to natural selection. About this same time, his concern with spiritualism became more demanding, and occupied a large part of his interest during the rest of his life. He showed some predilection for espousing unpopular causes. A socialist, he wrote in favor of land nationalization, and was an ardent antivaccinationist. Although he believed that his interest in spiritualism was an open-minded, scientific one, his own accounts of its revelations are far from convincing.

The story of his life as told by himself is replete with factual details, but singularly lacking, in general, in expression or description of his emotional reactions, except for his passion for fairness. He writes of the deaths of both parents, four sisters, and two brothers with no comments of a personal nature. A single sentence records his marriage to Miss Mitten, the eighteen-year-old eldest daughter of his friend Mr. William Mitten, the botanist. This occurred when he was forty-one.

One incident occurring during his stay in the Malay Archipelago is told with a peculiar whimsey and ambiguity which is exceptional for him. He relates his acquisition of an orphan baby which he had been nursing for more than a month, being responsible for the death of the mother. She was a wild woman whom he had mistaken for a monkey and shot when he saw her climbing around in a tree. The baby fell from her arms, almost literally into his. Without further explanation, he leaves his reader completely at sea as to whether the baby was human or monkey—or whether, in some fantasy state, he looked upon it as one of the "missing links" which were to concern him so much a few years later. It was surely monkey, for he later mentions its being at the zoo. (This summary is based largely on Wallace's *My Life*.)

13. In a conversation with Sir William Richmond, the painter, Darwin is reported to have said that without doubt the first three years were the most subject to incubative impressions. His explanation was based on the observation that "the brain at that period is entirely formed—a virgin brain adapted to receive impressions, and although unable to formulate or memorize these, they none-the-less remain and can affect the whole future life of the child recipient" (Stirling, 1926, p. 101).

14. In the autobiography of Edmund Gosse, we get a vivid glimpse of the havoc threatened by the impact of Darwin's theories on religiously inclined scientists. The elder Gosse, a moderately well-known botanist and member of the Plymouth Brethren, retreated staunchly from the heresy and enfolded himself more and more in the intricacies of morphological studies showing the infinite varieties of God's creation and adding to His glorification. (Edmund Gosse, *Father and Son*.)

15. T. H. Huxley, who was so intimately associated with Darwin, used the theme in "Agnosticism: A Rejoinder" (1889), and in general followed the arguments given by Butler, but did not mention him. But the theme occupied others as well. It was certainly presented in some form in Strauss's *Life of Jesus* even before Butler's pamphlet. It was later developed variously by Oscar

Wilde, Frank Harris, George Moore, D. H. Lawrence, H. L. Mencken, and doubtless some others. Only the Huxley article and perhaps the one by Frank Harris were published before Butler's death. Wilde never published his, though he embellished it much in an account to William Butler Yeats (W. B. Yeats's *Autobiography*, p. 119).

16. All during December, 1877, Butler was worried and carried on some correspondence about this with Francis Darwin and Miss Savage.

For unknown reasons, the publication date of *Life and Habit* is given as 1878 in all the biographies and in a bibliography of Butler's work, and even in the *Memoirs* by Jones (1919), the text of which explicitly says that it was published on December 4, 1877, which was Butler's birthday. It may not have been released until after January 1, 1878. The notes indicated that it was reviewed sometime before January 10, 1878. But on December 29, 1877, Butler was writing to Francis Darwin about his relief that the latter had not found the book "unpardonable."

17. Ewald Hering, physiologist and psychologist, lecturer at the University of Leipzig, in Vienna, in Prague, and then again in Leipzig. His chief work was in optics, especially the perception of color. In 1870 he published *Über das Gedächtnis als eine allgemeine Funktion der organisierten Materie*. Butler quoted an essay of Hering's on memory.

The Biographical Background of the Controversialists

18. That Robert Waring Darwin had had a difficult childhood is revealed in a letter from his father, Eras-

[106]

mus. It is apparent that at twenty-six Robert was reluctant to marry unless he understood more concerning the illness of his mother who had died when he was four. It would appear that the mother had bouts of pain followed by convulsions considered as hysterical by her husband. For these she took opium and alcohol, after which she would become delirious for a short time. The young boy witnessed these attacks and would sometimes run for help. These early crises may have contributed to his later interest in the marital troubles of his patients. (See "Letter of Erasmus Darwin to Robert Waring Darwin" in Appendix of the *Autobiography* of Charles Darwin, ed. Barlow [1958].)

19. A letter from Elizabeth Wedgwood describes the dreariness of a visit to The Mound, the home of the Robert W. Darwins, while the young people waited for the Tide to come in (Litchfield, 1915, 1:139).

20. Geoffrey West, one of the biographers of Charles Darwin, takes issue with any interpretation of Charles's childhood hobbies as having any particular significance either in relation to his later naturalist interest or in the development of his character. West, who seems opposed to recognizing emotional contributions to Charles Darwin's lifelong neurotic illness, considers these pursuits as merely such as every boy has at that age. The biographer would appear to consider a neurosis as a defect incompatible with the character of a great man (West, 1938).

21. See F. Darwin, ed., *Life and Letters of Charles Darwin,* 2:236.

22. *Ibid.,* 2:237.

23. *Ibid.,* 1:152.

24. *Autobiography of Charles Darwin,* ed. N. Barlow (1958). The interpretation regarding Charles's dilemma about sexual differences is elaborated in an early publication by E. J. Kempf (1920), and has aroused scornful criticism from Geoffrey West (1938). One can only wonder, however, in view of the obvious capacity of the child to repress and deny, whether this preoccupation with the flowers could also have been in part determined from his hearing anything about the publications of his grandfather, Erasmus, whose influence he was later to repudiate, but who late in life published his *Loves of the Plants,* which attained wide circulation. Certainly within a few years, while still at Shrewsbury School, Charles was reading some of his grandfather's books. Toward the end of his life, he was much preoccupied (again?) with the sex life of the flowers, and was writing on self-fertilization and cross-fertilization of certain species.

25. I. Hermann (1927) considers that the memory of the soldier was stronger than that of the mother, and represents a wish that the father rather than the mother should have died. This is certainly possible, but is less clear to me than the fact of the failure to remember the body of either, and the fixation, rather, on the trappings.

26. So great was his investment here that toward the end of his life he said: "When I am obliged to give up observation and experimenting I shall die." Even later he wrote to Wallace: "I have taken up old botanical work and given up all theories." Flowers, which had been so significant in the beginning of his infantile experiments with the "colored waters," remained his solace and his pets to the end of his life. One of his last publications was *The Different Forms of Flowers on Plants*

of the Same Species (1877), of which he writes in his autobiography (p. 134) that no discovery has given him so much pleasure as the making out of the meaning of heterostyled flowers; and again he remarks (p. 135): "It has always pleased me to exalt plants in the scale of organized beings," and "I felt an especial pleasure in showing how many and what admirably well-adapted movements the tip of a root possesses."

27. Professor John Stevens Henslow, geologist, botanist, professor of mineralogy after 1822, took holy orders in 1823 and in 1825 became professor of botany. In 1832 he became a vicar of Cholsey-cum-Moulsford, and in 1839 rector of Hitcham. He took a very great interest in Charles Darwin, whose talents he clearly recognized.

28. When Charles wrote his father, telling him of the opportuntiy of going as naturalist on the *Beagle* and asking for his backing, Dr. Robert Darwin objected vehemently, on the grounds that it was a wild scheme, a useless undertaking, which constituted a change in profession, or would at least be damaging to the character of a man who planned to become a clergyman; that it had probably been offered to someone else first, and the fact that no one else had accepted it indicated that there was probably something wrong with it anyway. In addition, the accomodations would be uncomfortable, and the trip would be generally unsettling. He did concede, however, that if Charles could present a single reasonable person who favored his going on the exploration, he, Dr. Robert, would reconsider his objections. Charles then discussed the matter with his Wedgwood cousins, who seemed generally to favor his going. It ended with "Uncle Jos" Wedgwood (Charles's future father-in-law and a man

much respected by Dr. Robert Darwin) writing such a letter in Charles's behalf that it turned the Tide in his favor (Barlow, 1958, pp. 220-230.)

29. In a recent discussion of the neurosis, one writer, Dr. Rankine Good (1954a), states that Darwin already had developed neurotic symptoms during a period at Cambridge before he had ever heard of the *Beagle;* but he does not give the nature and source of his evidence. From most accounts it appears that the symptoms of palpitation and fear of being invalided and unable to sail developed acutely during the time at Devonport when Darwin was waiting for the much-delayed sailing of the ship to take place.

30. See: *Charles Darwin and the Voyage of the "Beagle,"* ed. N. Barlow (1946).

31. For the full text of Darwin's argument *This is the Question* (i.e., whether or not to marry), see the *Autobiography of Charles Darwin,* ed. N. Barlow (1946, pp. 232-234).

32. He seemed surprised at his own feelings for a young baby. He wrote a friend: "He is so charming that I cannot pretend to any modesty. I defy anyone to flatter us on our baby, for I defy anyone to say anything in its praise of which we are not fully conscious. . . . I had not the smallest conception that there was so much in a five-month-old baby. You will perceive by this that I have a full degree of paternal fervor." (*Life and Letters of Charles Darwin,* ed. F. Darwin [1911, 1:270].)

33. Chief among these were the *Expression of the Emotions in Man and Animals* (1872), and the "Biography of an Infant" in *Mind* (1877).

[110]

34. This rather sad little life began and ended in a period of scientific and creative turmoil in the father's life, with which it merged and by which it later seemed overshadowed. The child was possibly defective, not having learned to walk or talk by the age of two. He died during an epidemic of scarlet fever, when another child was ill with diphtheria. Whether the father brooded about this or drew a merciful curtain again of denial cannot be told from the letters which are available. It is certainly striking that the Uncle Charles for whom Charles Darwin was named, and the son Charles who was named for him, both died young. But how he regarded this or whether he regarded it at all cannot be told (West, 1938, p. 230).

35. See Frontispiece in *Emma Darwin: A Century of Family Letters,* edited by her daughter, Henrietta Litchfield (1915).

36. *Ibid.,* 2:173, 175.

37. *Ibid.,* 1:140.

38. *Ibid.,* 2:145.

39. *Ibid.,* 2:246.

40. *Ibid.,* 2:310.

41. See remarks of Douglas Hubble regarding Emma Darwin's possible overmotherliness (1943, p. 129; 1946, p. 74; 1953, pp. 1351-1354; 1954, p. 467).

42. See *Samuel Butler, a Memoir,* by H. Festing Jones (1919, 1:9).

43. Mrs. Richard S. Garnett (Martha), who was related to Butler's mother, wrote a biography of Butler

after the posthumous publication of *The Way of All Flesh*. Her aim was to give the family's side of the picture, since she clearly felt that Butler had gone too far in lampooning his parents. Indirectly, however, she arouses some sympathy for the child growing up in his father's school, with a mother greatly absorbed in the father but with special anxiety that all should appear well (Garnett, 1926).

44. "He [father] never liked me, nor I him; from my earliest recollections I can call to mind no time when I did not fear him and dislike him. Over and over again I have relented toward him and said to myself that he was a good fellow after all; but I had hardly done so when he would go for me in some way or other which soured me again. I have no doubt that I made myself very disagreeable. . . . But no matter whose [fault] it is, the fact remains that for years and years I have not passed a day without thinking of him many times over as the man who was sure to be against me" (Jones, 1919, 1:20).

45. Jones (1919, 2:47).

46. See *The Earnest Atheist,* by Malcolm Muggeridge (1936).

47. See *Autobiography* of William B. Yeats (1938).

48. Butler's letter to his cousin, Philip J. Worsley, January 10, 1861: ". . . First let me congratulate you upon your own happy prospect. I am not in love myself, nor ever have been since certain spooney intervals as a boy. I have my ideal—and should I fall in with her shall recognize her at a glance, but as yet I have never done so. Still I can sympathize with those who have found the haven wherein their hearts can rest. My enemies doubt

whether I am possessed of such an inconvenient piece of lumber at all. I believe, however, that it exists. . . ."

To his aunt he wrote of his wish for a wife as a kind of superior and devoted servant. But he seemed to find that men served this role for him better than women (Jones, 1919, 1:96).

49. Jones (1919, 1:107).

50. *Ibid.*, 1:113.

51. *Ibid.*, 2:286-287.

52. *Ibid.*, 2:414.

53. He is reported to have said: "A good Butler is a dead Butler."

54. *Samuel Butler, the Incarnate Bachelor,* by Philip Henderson (1953, p. 79).

55. In regard to the noises: "he stayed so long [on the Continent in 1869] because of the continued growth of a tumour at the back of his neck and because of the increase in loud noises in his head when on the point of going to sleep, as though a violent charge were being made suddenly outside. The first few times the noise came, he got out of bed and went in to his sitting room to investigate, thinking that the crash had taken place there." The noises had begun in 1866. In December 1899, Butler wrote that both symptoms had long subsided. "The tumour and the noises are my storm-signals. When they show signs of returning it is time for me to slacken off work. Neither symptom became materially better until the death of my father and some time afterwards." (*Samuel Butler, a Memoir* by Jones [1919, 1:130].) In 1883, "All this spring, Butler was suffering from brain-

fag with a return of the crashes in his head just before going to sleep. He could not lessen the anxieties and worries arising from his financial difficulties, the strained relation with his father, and the anxieties in connection with Pauli" (*ibid.*, 1:384). In 1884, Butler was again writing—now to Festing Jones's brother Ted—concerning the noises (*ibid.*, 1:430). Canon Butler died in 1886.

56. For photographs, see Philip Henderson (1953, pp. 21-61); H. Festing Jones (1919, Vol. I, Frontispiece; 1:31, 45, 58; 2:64, 239, 282, 326).

57. Jones (1919, 2:205).

58. *Ibid.,* 2:204.

59. *Ibid.,* 2:236; see also Jones (1912, p. 249).

60. He found that Colonel Mure in his *Language and Literature of Antient Greece* had developed the theme somewhat (Jones, 1919, 2:121). More recently, the same opinion has been expressed by Robert Graves (1955).

61. Jones (1919, 2:439-440).

62. *Ibid.,* 1:284.

63. *Ibid.,* 2:128.

64. See Muggeridge (1936).

65. Jones (1919, 2:414).

References

Alvarez, W. C. (1943), The Asthma of Charles Darwin and Its Cause. In: *Nervousness, Indigestion and Pain.* New York & London: Paul Hoeber, pp. 240-243.

Ashmun, M. E. (1931), *The Singing Swan.* New Haven: Yale Univ. Press.

Barlow, N., ed. (1946), *Charles Darwin and the Voyage of the "Beagle."* New York: Philosophical Library.

—— (1954), On Darwin (continuing The Life of the Shawl). *Lancet,* 266:414-415.

——, ed. (1958), *The Autobiography of Charles Darwin* (Complete Version). London: Collins.

Bibby, C. (1959), *T. H. Huxley: Scientist, Humanist and Educator.* New York: Horizon Press.

Butler, S. (1863), Darwin Among the Machines. New Zealand: *The Press,* Part VI, No. 6 (June 13).

—— (1865a), Lucubratio Ebria. New Zealand: *The Press,* Part II, No. 9 (July 29).

—— (1865b), *Resurrection of Jesus Christ.* London: published anonymously.

—— (1872), *Erewhon.* London: Trübner and Co.

—— (1873), *The Fair Haven.* London: Trübner and Co.

—— (1877), *Life and Habit.* London: Trübner and Co., 1878.

[115]

—— (1879), *Evolution Old and New: Theories of Buffon, Dr. Erasmus Darwin and Lamarck as Compared with That of Mr. Charles Darwin*. London: Hardwicke and Bogue.

—— (1880), *Unconscious Memory*. London: David Bogue.

—— (1896), *Life and Letters of Dr. Samuel Butler* [his grandfather], 2 Vols. London: John Murray.

—— (1897), *The Authoress of the Odyssey*. London: Longmans, Green & Co.

—— (1903), *The Way of All Flesh*. London: Grant Richards.

Carlyle, T. (1881), *Reminiscences,* ed. James Anthony Froude. New York: Charles Scribner's Sons, p. 433.

Cole, G. D. H. (1948), *Samuel Butler*. Denver: Alan Swallow.

Comfort, A. (1960), Darwin and Freud. *Lancet,* July 16, 1960, pp. 107-111.

—— (1961), *Darwin and the Naked Lady*. Chap. 2: Darwin and Freud. London: Routledge and Kegan Paul, pp. 23-43.

Darlington, C. D. (1959), The Origin of Darwinism. *Scientific American,* 200:60-66.

Darwin, C. (1859), *On the Origin of Species by Means of Natural Selection*. London: John Murray.

—— (1871), *The Descent of Man and Selection in Relation to Sex*. London: John Murray, 2 vols.

—— (1872), *The Expression of the Emotions in Man and Animals*. London: John Murray.

—— (1877), Biography of an Infant. In: *Mind,* 2:285-294.

Darwin, F., ed. (1911), *Life and Letters of Charles Darwin,* 2 Vols. New York & London: D. Appleton & Co.

[116]

—— (1912), Fitzroy and Darwin. In: *Nature,* February 22, 1912, pp. 547-548.

Eiseley, L. (1961), *Darwin's Century.* Garden City: Doubleday and Co.

Freud, S. (1910), Leonardo da Vinci and a Memory of His Childhood. *Standard Edition,* 11:59-137. London: Hogarth Press, 1957.

—— (1930 [1929]), Civilization and Its Discontents. *Standard Edition,* 21:59-145. London: Hogarth Press, 1957.

Garnett, M. (1926), *Samuel Butler and His Family Relations.* London, Toronto, & New York: J. M. Dent and Sons, Ltd.

Good, R. (1954a), The Origin of the Origin. In: *Biology and Human Affairs,* 20:10-16.

—— (1954b), On Darwin. *Lancet,* 266:106-107.

Gosse, E. W. (1907), *Father and Son.* New York: C. Scribner's Sons.

Graves, R. (1955), *Homer's Daughter.* New York: Doubleday & Co.

Gray, A. (1876), *Darwiniana.* New York: D. Appleton and Co.

Greenacre, P. (1956), Experiences of Awe in Childhood. *The Psychoanalytic Study of the Child,* 11:9-30. New York: Int. Univ. Press.

—— (1957), The Childhood of the Artist. *The Psychoanalytic Study of the Child,* 12:47-72. New York: Int. Univ. Press.

Greene, J. C. (1961), *Darwin and the Modern World View.* Baton Rouge: Louisiana State Univ. Press.

Harris, J. F. (1916), *Samuel Butler, Author of Erewhon: the Man and His Work.* New York: Dodd, Mead and Co.

Henderson, P. (1953), *Samuel Butler: the Incarnate Bachelor.* London: Cohen and West, Ltd.

Hermann, I. (1927), Charles Darwin. *Imago,* 13:57-82.

Hubble, D. (1943), Charles Darwin and Psychotherapy. *Lancet,* 244:129.

—— (1946), The Evolution of Charles Darwin. *Horizon,* 80:74.

—— (1953), The Life of the Shawl. *Lancet,* 263:1351-1354.

—— (1954), Again the Life of the Shawl. *Lancet,* 266:467.

Huxley, T. H. (1889), Agnosticism: A Rejoinder. *The Nineteenth Century,* 25:700-721.

—— (1893), *Darwiniana.* New York: D. Appleton and Co.

Johnston, W. W. (1901), The Ill Health of Charles Darwin. *American Anthropologist,* 3:139-158.

Jones, H. F., ed. (1912), *The Note Books of Samuel Butler.* London: Fifield.

—— (1919), *Samuel Butler: a Memoir,* 2 Vols. London: Macmillan and Co., Ltd.

Kempf, E. J. (1920), *Psychopathology.* St. Louis: C. V. Mosby and Co.

Krause, E. (1879), *Erasmus Darwin, with a preliminary notice by Charles Darwin.* London: John Murray. Revised: New York: D. Appleton and Co., 1880.

Kris, E. (1952), *Psychoanalytic Explorations in Art.* New York: Int. Univ. Press.

Litchfield, H., ed. (1915), *Emma Darwin: a Century of Family Letters,* 2 Vols. London: John Murray.

Muggeridge, M. (1936), *The Earnest Atheist.* London: Eyre and Spottiswoode.

Mure, W. (1850–1857), *A Critical History of the Lan-*

guage and Literature of Antient Greece, 5 Vols. London: Longman, Brown, Green and Longmans.

Raverat, Gwen (1952), *Period Piece.* London: Faber, 1960.

Seward, A. (1804), *Life of Dr. Darwin.* Philadelphia: Classics Press for William Poyntill and Co.

Seward, A. C. (1909), *Darwin and Modern Science.* Cambridge: Cambridge Univ. Press.

Shaw, G. B. (1905), *Major Barbara.* Preface. Baltimore: Penguin Books, 1959.

—— (1921), *Back to Methuselah.* Preface: The Infidel Half Century. New York: Brentano's.

Silver, A. (1962), *The Family Letters of Samuel Butler.* London: Jonathan Cape.

Spencer, H. (1884), *An Autobiography,* 2 Vols. London: William and Norgate.

Stillman, C. G. (1932), *Samuel Butler, a Mid-Victorian Modern.* London: Martin Secker.

Stirling, A. M. W. (1926), *The Richmond Papers.* London: William Heinemann.

Strachey, L. (1921), *Queen Victoria.* New York: Harcourt, Brace and Co.

Wallace, A. R. (1905), *My Life: a Record of Events and Opinions,* 2 Vols. New York: Dodd, Mead and Co.

West, G. (1938), *Charles Darwin.* New Haven: Yale Univ. Press.

Willey, B. (1959), *Darwin and Butler: Two Versions of Evolution.* New York: Harcourt, Brace and Co., 1960.

Yeats, J. B. (1917), Recollections of Samuel Butler. *Seven Arts,* 2, Aug. 1917.

Yeats, W. B. (1938), *Autobiography.* New York: Macmillan Co.

Phyllis Greenacre, M.D.

A native of Chicago, Illinois (born 1894), Dr. Greenacre was educated there in the public elementary and
high schools, attended the University of Chicago and
Rush Medical College. Although she early had a
definite interest in and plan of working in the field
of psychiatry, her first special training was in general
pathology. The eleven years (1916–1927) were spent
in the Department of Psychiatry of the Johns Hopkins
Hospital and Medical School in Baltimore, on the
resident and teaching staff and engaged in some
studies in neurosyphilis. From 1927 to 1932 she was
Psychiatric Consultant to the child care division of
the Department of Public Welfare of Westchester
County (New York). Then followed thirty years of
affiliation with the Department of Psychiatry of New
York Hospital and Cornell Medical College, first as
an assistant professor and then as professor of clinical
psychiatry. Until 1946 she was active in teaching and
in the direction of the Psychiatric Outpatient Service;
in later years she served only as an occasional consultant.

She became a member of the New York Psychoanalytic Society and Institute in 1937, and since 1942 has been a member of its faculty. Dr. Greenacre served as President of the Institute from 1948 to 1950, and as President of the Society from 1956 to 1957. She has given the Freud Anniversay Lecture in 1953, the Brill Lecture in 1956, and the Mirviss Memorial Lecture (in San Francisco) in 1959, as well as the Alexander Lecture of the Chicago Psychoanalytic Institute in the same year. She was a recipient of the Blackwell Award in 1955 and of the Menninger Award in 1959.

In 1927 she began the practice of psychiatry in New York, and since 1937 has devoted herself largely to psychoanalytic practice, and has contributed to clinical research in psychoanalysis. Her interests there have been focused chiefly on studies of infantile development in relation to the genesis of later neurotic disorders; and more recently on biographical studies in connection with an investigation into problems of the creative individual.

Publications by Dr. Greenacre

1917

Multiple Spontaneous Intracerebral Hemorrhages. *The Johns Hopkins Hospital Bulletin,* 28:1-10.

1918

The Content of Schizophrenic Characteristics Occurring in Affective Disorders. *American Journal of Insanity,* 75:197-202.

1923

A Study of the Mechanism of Obsessive-Compulsive Conditions. *American Journal of Psychiatry,* 2:527-538.

1926

The Eye Motif in Delusion and Fantasy. *American Journal of Psychiatry,* 5:553-580.

1932

How Shall We Decide What Kind of Care to Give to Our Dependent Children. *Quarterly Bulletin of the New York State Conference on Social Work.*

1933

Consideration of the Role of the Father in Treatment of a Mother's Aid Situation. *Family,* 13:291-299.

1935

Special Problems in Boarding Home Work. *Family,* 16: 48-53.

1939

Surgical Addiction—A Case Illustration. *Psychosomatic Medicine,* 1:325-328.

1941

The Predisposition to Anxiety, Part I. *The Psychoanalytic Quarterly,* 10:66-95.

The Predisposition to Anxiety, Part II. *The Psychoanalytic Quarterly,* 10:610-637.

1944

Infant Reactions to Restraint: Problems in the Fate of Infantile Aggression. *American Journal of Orthopsychiatry,* 14:204-218; also in *Trauma, Growth and Personality,* pp. 83-105.

1945

Conscience in the Psychopath. *American Journal of Orthopsychiatry,* 15:495-509; also in *Trauma, Growth and Personality,* pp. 165-187.

Urination and Weeping. *American Journal of Orthopsychiatry,* 15:81-88; also in *Trauma, Growth and Personality,* pp. 106-119.

Biological Economy of Birth. *The Psychoanalytic Study of the Child,* 1:31-53. New York: Int. Univ. Press; also in *Trauma, Growth and Personality,* pp. 3-26.

Pathological Weeping. *The Psychoanalytic Quarterly,* 14:62-75; also in *The Yearbook of Psychoanalysis,* 2:117-130, New York: Int. Univ. Press, 1946; *Trauma, Growth and Personality,* pp. 120-131.

1946

Training for Teaching Psychiatry. Symposium. *American Journal of Orthopsychiatry,* 16:413-417.

1947

Child Wife as Ideal: Sociological Considerations. *American Journal of Orthopsychiatry,* 17:167-171.

Vision, Headache and Halo: Reactions to Stress in the Course of Superego Formation. *The Psychoanalytic Quarterly,* 16:177-194; also in *Trauma, Growth and Personality,* pp. 132-148.

Problems of Patient-Therapist Relationships in the Treatment of Psychopaths. *Handbook of Correctional Psychoanalysis,* ed. R. M. Lindner, & R. V. Seliger. New York: Philosophical Library, pp. 378-383.

1948

Evaluation of Therapeutic Results. Symposium. *The International Journal of Psycho-Analysis,* 29:7-33; also in *The Yearbook of Psychoanalysis,* 5:11-34, New York: Int. Univ. Press, 1949.

Anatomical Structure and Superego Development. *American Journal of Orthopsychiatry,* 18:636-648; also in *Trauma, Growth, and Personality,* pp. 149-164.

1949

Social Applications of Psychiatry in Adolescence. *Social Medicine, Its Derivatives and Objectives,* ed. Iago Galston. New York: Commonwealth Fund, pp. 249-255.

A Contribution to the Study of Screen Memories. *The Psychoanalytic Study of the Child,* 3/4:73-84. New York: Int. Univ. Press; also in *Trauma, Growth and Personality,* pp. 188-203.

A Genetic Approach to the Problem of Inconsistency of Social Attitudes. *Journal of Social Issues,* 5:19-26.

1950

General Problems of Acting Out. *The Psychoanalytic Quarterly,* 19:455-467; also in *Trauma, Growth and Personality,* pp. 224-236.

Special Problems of Early Female Sexual Development. *The Psychoanalytic Study of the Child,* 5:112-138; also in *Trauma, Growth and Personality,* pp. 237-258.

1951

The Prepuberty Trauma in Girls. *The Psychoanalytic Quarterly,* 19:298-317; also in *The Yearbook of Psychoanalysis,* 7:159-174. New York: Int. Univ. Press, 1951; *Trauma, Growth and Personality,* pp. 204-223.

Adolescence [The New York Academy of Medicine, Proceedings of Eastern States Health Education Conference]. *Psychological Dynamics of Health Education.* New York: Columbia Univ. Press, pp. x-134.

An Appraisal of Psychoanalysis for the Practitioner. *Bulletin of the New York Academy of Medicine,* 27:295-308.

Respiratory Incorporation and the Phallic Phase. *The Psychoanalytic Study of the Child,* 6:180-205. New York: Int. Univ. Press; also in *Trauma, Growth and Personality,* pp. 259-292.

1952

Pregenital Patterning. *The International Journal of Psycho-Analysis,* 33:410-415.

Some Factors Producing Different Types of Genital and Pregenital Organization. *Trauma, Growth and Personality,* pp. 293-302.

Trauma, Growth and Personality. New York: W. W. Norton, xii+328 pp.

1953

Psychoanalysis and the Cycles of Life. *The Bulletin of the New York Academy of Medicine,* 29:796-810.

Certain Relationships between Fetishism and the Faulty Development of the Body Image. *The Psychoanalytic Study of the Child,* 8:79-98. New York: Int. Univ. Press.

Penis Awe and Its Relation to Penis Envy. *Drives, Affects, Behavior,* ed. R. M. Loewenstein. New York: Int. Univ. Press, pp. 176-190.

Affective Disorders, ed. Phyllis Greenacre. New York: Int. Univ. Press, 212 pp.

1954

The Role of Transference; Practical Considerations in Relation to Psychoanalytic Therapy. *Journal of the American Psychoanalytic Association,* 2:671-684.

Problems of Infantile Neurosis: a Discussion. *The Psychoanalytic Study of the Child,* 9:16-71. New York: Int. Univ. Press.

1955

Further Considerations Regarding Fetishism. *The Psychoanalytic Study of the Child,* 10:187-194. New York: Int. Univ. Press.

The Mutual Adventures of Jonathan Swift and Lemuel Gulliver. *The Psychoanalytic Quarterly,* 24:20-62.

"It's My Own Invention"—A Special Screen Memory of Mr. Lewis Carroll; Its Form and Its History. *The Psychoanalytic Quarterly,* 24:200-244.

Swift and Carroll: A Psychoanalytic Study of Two Lives. New York: Int. Univ. Press, 306 pp.

1956

Experiences of Awe in Childhood. *The Psychoanalytic Study of the Child,* 11:9-30. New York: Int. Univ. Press.

Re-evaluation of the Process of Working Through. *The International Journal of Psycho-Analysis,* 37:439-444.

1957

The Childhood of the Artist: Libidinal Phase Development and Giftedness. *The Psychoanalytic Study of the Child,* 12:47-72. New York: Int. Univ. Press.

1958

The Impostor. *The Psychoanalytic Quarterly.* 27:359-382.

The Family Romance of the Artist. *The Psychoanalytic Study of the Child,* 13:9-43. New York: Int. Univ. Press.

The Relation of the Impostor to the Artist. *The Psychoanalytic Study of the Child,* 13:521-540. New York: Int. Univ. Press.

Early Physical Determinants in the Development of the Sense of Identity. *Journal of the American Psychoanalytic Association,* 4:612-627.

Toward an Understanding of the Physical Nucleus of Some Defence Reactions. *The International Journal of Psycho-Analysis,* 39:1-8.

1959

On Focal Symbiosis. *Dynamic Psychopathology in Childhood,* ed. L. Jessner & E. Pavenstedt. New York: Grune & Stratton, pp. 243-256.

Certain Technical Problems in the Transference Relationship. *Journal of the American Psychoanalytic Association,* 7:484-502.

Play in Relation to Creative Imagination. *The Psychoanalytic Study of the Child,* 14:61-80. New York: Int. Univ. Press.

1960

Woman as Artist. *The Psychoanalytic Quarterly,* 29:208-227.

Regression and Fixation: Considerations Concerning the Development of the Ego. *Journal of the American Psychoanalytic Association,* 8:703-723.

Further Notes on Fetishism. *The Psychoanalytic Study of the Child,* 15:191-207. New York: Int. Univ. Press.

Considerations Regarding the Parent-Infant Relationship. *The International Journal of Psycho-Analysis,* 61:571-584.

1961

A Critical Digest of the Literature on Selection of Candidates for Psychoanalytic Training. *The Psychoanalytic Quarterly,* 30:28-55.

Quelques considérations sur la relation parent-nourisson. *La Revue Française de Psychanalyse,* 25:27-53.

1962

The Early Years of the Gifted Child: a Psychoanalytic Interpretation. *1962 Yearbook of Education.* New York: Harcourt, Brace, & World.

Discussion and Comments on the Psychology of Creativity. *Journal of the American Academy of Child Psychiatry,* 1:129-137.

1963

Problems of Acting Out in the Transference Relationship. *Journal of the Academy of Child Psychiatry,* (in press).